How to Run Your Own Life

How to Run Your Own Life

by Jut Meininger

Grosset & Dunlap
A Filmways Company
Publishers   New York

Acknowledgments

THIS BOOK WOULD not have been written without the considerable help and encouragement of Jim Barnett, who understood the Martian right from the beginning. It would never have been completed without the total involvement of my wife Elissa, who worked so hard that some of the pages are more hers than my own.

*To Elissa, who's a shining
example of how all this works*

Contents

The Beginning

The Secret

FORTY YEARS AGO Dr. Napoleon Hill, in his famous book *Think and Grow Rich,* outlined in detail the process by which hundreds of the most successful men of the century had obtained financial wealth and personal happiness. His book was a total immersion course on how to get rich and lead a contented life. To this day it remains unequaled. It contains virtually all the information needed to achieve success in life. Yet of the tens of millions of people who've read it, only a handful have ever become rich.

For those who have, little else was needed. Yet, as Dr. Hill himself so aptly put it, a person must be prepared to use such information, or it will be of little value to him. He must be *ready* to take advantage of it, or he won't know what to do with it. Unfortunately, very few people have been able to reach that state of readiness.

Why is this? Why, with so many searching for wealth and happiness, do so few find it? Why, of all those hoping to learn from Dr. Hill's book, have so few ever been ready? And, if it's possible to tell someone how to get rich once he's ready, why isn't it possible to tell him how to *become* ready?

These questions have puzzled me for years. Only recently have I understood the answers clearly enough to share them with others.

The average person usually decides to become rich and happy after years of operating his life in ways that *prevent* him from becoming rich and happy. By the time he's interested in learning how to get rich, he's already doing things—working, playing, studying, and organizing his life—on the basis of earlier decisions. He's usually left himself little room in which to add new ways of doing things to the ones he already employs.

He's already decided, for instance, what he likes to do, what he doesn't like to do; what comes easy to him, what comes hard; what's fun, what's work; what he's willing to settle for, what he's *not* willing to settle for; what he expects of himself, what he expects of others; what he's attracted to, what he's repelled by; how to get what he wants, and whether or not he *can* get what he wants; how to make enemies, how to make friends; how to please people, and whether or not he *can* please people; how to get people to do things for him; how to succeed, how to fail; how to become accepted, and whether or not he *can* be accepted; the types of people he likes; the types of activities he likes; whether or not he's going places in life, and whether or not he is stuck.

He's also made other, more "practical" decisions about where he'll go to school; whom he'll marry; where he'll live; how many children he'll have; whether he'll save money or spend it; whether he'll strike out on his own or play it safe; whether he'll have a small home or a large one; whether he'll keep up with the Joneses or ignore them; whether he'll do—or not do—any of the things people normally start thinking about as they're growing up.

By the time the average person even *thinks* about deciding to become rich and happy, he's harnessed himself with so many decisions on such a wide range of issues affecting his life that it's almost impossible for him to make a new decision that doesn't conflict in some way with the ones he's already operating from. He's overloaded! There's almost no way he can make use of any more information—regardless of how good it is, and regardless of where it comes from!

He can't just pick up a book on how to do something with his life and immediately put it to use. He can't go around looking for new information, or new instructions on how to do things, and expect them to supplement those he's already operating from. They won't! There's no way they can! (At least not very often.) New instructions rarely *supplement* earlier ones. They more likely *conflict* with them! And when new instructions conflict with what someone's already doing, his older instructions and earlier decisions will continue to take precedence, simply because he's never done anything to alter them.

But this no longer means the average person can't become rich and happy! It just means he can't do so by using any of the old methods (which never worked, anyway)! Before picking up a new book, and before looking for new instructions, he must first *prepare* himself. He must get himself *ready* to use those instructions before they can be of any help to him!

How can he do that? Or, better yet, how can *you*? Well, the secret of getting ready lies not in learning new instructions, but in canceling out some of the instructions you're already operating from. It lies not in learning *more* things to do, but in learning to *stop* doing the things you're already doing that stand in your way. It lies not in making new decisions, but in redeciding the decisions you've already made that prevent you from doing what you *now* want to do!

And how do you find out which decisions you need to redecide? How do you learn what you need to stop doing? While there's no way someone can *tell* you what you need to stop doing, there's a *process* you can learn that will enable you to find out for yourself. It's something anyone can learn, if he's interested enough to give it his constant attention. Before describing the process, however, I'd like to take a moment and look at how we go about making these early decisions that later stand in our way so you can get an idea of what you're up against when you undertake the task of redeciding them.

The Life Plan*

All of us build our lives pretty much the same way. We pick up information about ourselves and the world around us, and use this information to make decisions about all aspects of our lives. We start doing this almost from birth. Many of our most important decisions are based on what others say to us and how they treat us during the first four or five years of our life. The information we receive is, of course, limited to what a small child can see and hear within his immediate environment, and the possibilities for distortion are enormous. Yet in spite of its limitations and inaccuracies, this information forms the basis for some of our most important life decisions.

Our most significant information usually comes from our mother and father. Their words and actions have an especially large impact on us. Everything they say and do adds up to a mental image we use to shape our personalities and make major decisions about our entire lives. A child with the best possible genetic equipment can be permanently turned off to life through inaccurate information he receives from his parents. ("You're a dummy." "You're no good." "Nobody loves you." "You can't make it.") And a child with even the most modest possibilities can be made to blossom.

The first four to five years are critical to a youngster's development for several reasons. First, we all make certain broad-based decisions during this time which we use as building blocks for other decisions on down the road (our conclusions about ourselves and our ability to deal with others are perhaps the most important). Second, we experience many of these earlier decisions not as decisions at all, but rather as absolutes—as unchangeable rules of thumb about how the world really is! ("That's the way life

---

*For a more comprehensive explanation of life plans, see Claude Steiner's excellent book, *Scripts People Live* (New York: Grove Press, 1974).

is." "That's the way *I* am." "That's the way *people* are." "This is what I can expect to get out of life.") Once we consider them absolutes, these decisions are hard to alter later in life, even if we discover they're getting in our way. As building blocks for future decisions, they often distort later conclusions we make on really important issues such as what we'll strive for, what we'll settle for, how hard we'll try, and how long we'll persevere in life.

Whatever the basis for these decisions (whether our information is true or false, accurate or inaccurate), we simply can't avoid making them. It's part of the process of growing up. Soon we're piling many *more* decisions on top of them! All of these decisions, taken together, form a comprehensive plan for operating our lives. As time passes, they become second nature to us, and we no longer think of them as decisions. We see them more as an easily accepted method of operation that has always been with us. We take them for granted. And although they comprise a well-laid plan for living the rest of our life, we soon lose touch with the fact that there *is* a plan in operation—let alone one which we ourselves fully devised and set in motion.

All of us do this, whether we become hardened criminals, millionaire businessmen, derelict alcoholics, or contented housewives. There's no logic to the process; it just happens this way. What we don't realize when we're laying the groundwork for our own plan is that we're small of stature, limited in experience, dependent on others, and operating solely from the perspective of a young, less-than-fully-developed person. Yet the plan itself is meant to last a lifetime, and there's usually no built-in way to update it.

As you may have guessed, our life plan often determines whether we'll succeed or fail in life. People who succeed in *any* life endeavor operate from a different type of plan than that used by those who don't succeed. They employ a plan that at least *permits* success, even if it doesn't always contain specific career goals. These people consistently act as if they *have* a plan, and they constantly examine and alter their plan to keep pace with their conscious intentions.

Those who don't succeed in life operate from a different kind of plan—one that *prevents* success. They typically deny its existence (act as if they don't have a plan), and when confronted with the possibility that it might exist, they respond with fear and immobilize themselves, or with anger and become defensive. (Or, sometimes, by becoming confused or mindless, or by feeling empty or depressed.) They prevent themselves from examining their plan and thus avoid possibilities for alterations or change. Their plan may, in fact, selectively *exclude* such things as wealth and happiness. They may have decided *not* to feel happy or make money! (Perhaps because they "learned" that they couldn't do it, or perhaps because it threatened the "big" people in their family who were poor and unhappy themselves and resented others who weren't.) Without access to their own plan, and without a method for examining and changing it, they doom themselves to a lifetime of relative unhappiness and poverty.

The Dilemma

Most of us operate at one time or another from a life plan that no longer fits our conscious intentions. We make decisions in our youth that no longer serve us as adults. We grow up and find ourselves doing things or acting in ways that produce results different from those we intended. We often find it impossible to redirect our thoughts and actions in a comprehensive fashion to achieve our goals. For most of us, this represents a totally unsolvable dilemma.

Our life plan is often apparent only in retrospect—although, even then, we usually don't think of it as a "plan." We look back and we see what we've done, and we recognize a pattern or a certain compulsiveness about our behavior that we've had trouble arresting or gaining control over, and we're puzzled by it. But the plan itself is still very illusive. We see only its shadow-image. We see the *results* of our behavior, but not the decisions that *caused* it. Even when we occasionally guess the long-term implications of our plan and sense the possibility of an outcome we may not like, we usually experience the outcome as beyond our control. We don't recognize that *ours* are the hands that have been at the controls from the very beginning!

Sometimes we're clever at concealing our real decisions. We may *say* we want to become happy, and appear to work at it, yet remain unhappy. We may *act* as if we're trying to get rich, and make some apparent effort toward it, yet remain poor. Our plan may be to talk a good story, or to develop the outward appearance of doing one thing, while, in fact, we're doing something else. For a while we may fool others as well as ourselves. But eventually, our plan will become obvious as our life slowly unfolds—for a person's life is a *reflection* of his plan. It's the medium he uses to put his decisions into effect. The trick is to learn what these decisions are before they're confirmed by unwanted future events.

If you decided at some time in your life to make changes in how you go about things, you may already have a sense of how your existing plan conflicts with your goal of success. You may have found that you've surrounded yourself with people who influence you and who disapprove of your changes. You may have noticed that their approval was especially important to you, that you have trouble proceeding without it. You may have found that you've made a large investment in your present way of doing things, and that your mind is full of myths about the world around you, which you must sort through to find the ones that really make sense.

You may also have discovered that no sooner do you make a decision to feel happier and become richer than you start finding ways to stop yourself—at fairly predictable points and for fairly predictable reasons. You may notice you've developed great internal resistance to certain types of change, and that it's often a struggle just to keep going. You may become fearful, scared, anxious, or depressed. You may have an almost irresistible urge to lapse back into old patterns and return to the old ways. If you do, you're not alone. This sort of resistance is universal. It surfaces whenever someone decides to make a change in his life that runs counter to his basic life plan. The resistance is the signal that the plan itself is being tampered with.

The dilemma for most people, then, is twofold. Not only is their plan difficult to isolate, but it has its own built-in mechanism to prevent change! Together, these two obstacles have prevented millions of people from gaining power over their lives. Although formidable, these obstacles are not insurmountable.

The Process

Which brings us back to the question asked earlier: How can *you* isolate your own life plan, and recognize the decisions you've made that need changing? In addition: How can you overcome the internal resistance you'd normally experience in trying to change what you're doing?

Well, you can learn which decisions you need to change simply by *observing your current behavior*. Since your present behavior is a reflection of your earlier decisions about how to operate your life, by carefully watching what you do, by seeing where your actions lead, and by recognizing the attitudes and decisions these actions seem to reflect, you can get an extremely accurate idea of what your earlier decisions really were. At the point where you actually *change* those early decisions, the resistance you'd normally feel toward altering your life course will simply disappear, because there will be no conflict between your old decisions and your new ones.

This sounds somewhat easier than it is. You have to learn new ways to watch yourself, and new ways to examine your behavior. It's a skill that takes practice, but it can be mastered by virtually anyone, and it takes no special education, background, or intelligence.

If the process seems complicated to you at times, or

difficult to follow, remember that you didn't start out in life with a plan that led directly to riches and happiness. If you had, you'd already be rich and happy. Instead, you're involved in the process of *altering* an existing life plan—one that has its own momentum and direction—and this is not nearly as simple and direct a route to riches and happiness as starting from scratch. It involves both slowing down the momentum and changing the direction of your existing plan. It involves reversing certain decisions, altering others, and canceling out still others before any new, more functional decisions can be inserted in their place.

This book is devoted to demonstrating this process. It is arranged largely in the form of a dialogue between two people, interspersed with explanations to help keep you on track. To get the most out of the book, you must immerse yourself in the process itself, as if you were actually going through it. You must be willing to take the time, and make the effort, to become personally involved in the process as you are reading. *It will be your own responsibility to make the connections between the problems discussed in the dialogues and those you encounter in your own life.* The purpose of this book is not to solve your problems. It's to provide you with a method by which you can solve them yourself.

There are only two characters in the book: an Earth Person and a Martian. The Earth Person is a composite of many people. You'll see yourself in many of his struggles and triumphs, and you'll be able to experience how he goes about changing the way he operates his life. The Martian represents clarity—that is, the ability to see and hear things without prejudice or distortion. (This is an extension of an approach originally used by Eric Berne, who developed the notion of "Martian thinking."*) Coming from another planet, the Martian has no instructions about what things on earth "mean," and he makes no assumptions about the implications of what he observes. He sees and hears without

---

*See Eric Berne, *What Do You Say After You Say Hello?* (New York: Grove Press, 1972), p. 100.

distorting or coloring his perceptions with prejudice. He is subject to none of the usual confusions besetting Earth People, and he provides a totally unbiased sounding board for the Earth Person to use in examining his life plan, changing his old decisions, and formulating his new way of life.

Keep in mind that the Martian has no exceptional skills or talents. He has no great wisdom and no magical powers. He merely sees and hears things as they actually occur, with absolute clarity. The only skill *you* need to change your life, once you have the desire to do so, is this ability to see and hear clearly. Once you can do this, all the early decisions you'll need to change will become clearly apparent to you. Neither you nor anyone who helps you need be blessed with infinite wisdom or cosmic insight. You need nothing beyond the capabilities of the average human being. If you want to change your life, you can. The tools are now in your hands. You can become as rich and as happy as you want. The rest is up to you. I wish you the very best of luck.

CHAPTER ONE

EP Meets the Martian

EARTH PERSON: (Looking up suddenly) Hello! Who are you?

Martian: I'm a Martian.

EP: (Frowning) What are you doing here?

M: I've always been with you.

EP: Aw, cut it out. You really don't expect me to believe that, do you?

M: Believe me or not. That's your choice.

EP: (Stubbornly) Then how come I haven't seen you before?

M: You haven't been ready.

EP: What do you mean by that?

M: You're at a point in your life where what you've been taught and what you've been aware of aren't enough. You want more out of life than you know how to get.

EP: (More puzzled than defensive) But I still don't understand why I see you all of a sudden.

M: It's because you've started looking. You've started seeing things of value. You're lucky! Most people limit themselves to seeing things that aren't of any value to them.

EP: I don't get it! You mean seeing a Martian is *valuable*?

M: Very much so. I'm the key to all riches. I represent

21

your ability to see clearly. With clarity, there are no unob-
tainable goals.

EP: (Struggling to make sense of it all) So you, and clarity,
are one and the same?

M: That's right.

EP: But your being a Martian still seems kind of crazy to
me.

M: If you're willing to put aside your doubts about me for
a while, you'll soon understand who I am.

EP: (Hesitating) I guess it couldn't hurt. I've tried everything else. I could sure use some clarity right now, the way
my life's been going.

M: How's it been going?

EP: (Speaking sadly) Well, I used to think everything
would work out just fine, but it simply hasn't. I don't know
what's happened to my life. I'm just not getting anywhere!

M: Things are pretty bad, huh?

EP: (Looking depressed) Every now and then I'd like to
chuck it all. Even my marriage isn't what it *could* be.

M: I know. I've watched your life from the very beginning. I've seen how much unhappiness and confusion
you've brought on yourself.

EP: (Looking surprised) You mean you've been watching
me since I was born?

M: Right from the start.

EP: Well, how come you never said anything?

M: I tried often, but you never heard me. You weren't
ready. It's only recently that you started wondering how
you got yourself into this confused state. Before, you never
questioned it.

EP: I guess I didn't, did I?

M: No. But that's not unusual. Most Earth People live
their entire lives without ever stopping to see clearly.

EP: Really? You mean everybody else is in the same boat I
am?

M: Almost everyone. Most Earth People don't have the
faintest idea what they're doing, or where they're going in
life.

EP: Well, I know what *I'm* doing. I'm living a messed-up life.

M: You see only the *result* of what you're doing, not the process.

EP: Process? What do you mean, "process"?

M: Living is a process of making decisions about how to run your life, and then acting out those decisions. It's a process that never stops. You've made many decisions to bring yourself to your present point in life.

EP: (Defensively) Huh? I didn't make *decisions* to get myself into this position! Things just happened this way!

M: That's not what I saw. All along the way, you were the one who pulled the strings. If you recall, *you* decided who and when you would marry. *You* decided what job to take. *You* decided when to spend your money. No one else did this for you. Even when you were a child, you were making your own decisions.

EP: (Emphatically) Well, I certainly don't *remember* making any!

M: You may not remember making them, but you made them nevertheless. Many were not decisions in the normal sense of the word. Some were not even made consciously. Yet they were all decisions in the sense that before making them you were uncertain and kept questioning, and *after* making them you were certain of yourself and acted decisively.

EP: (Looking puzzled) I still don't understand.

M: Every action you took as a youngster was based on some internal assessment you made that it wouldn't harm you, that it seemed logical, and that it might also do you some good. *Every* action! Until you were sure of this, you didn't act.

EP: That makes sense. Don't all children do that?

M: Absolutely. It's the process on which they build their lives. But many of the decisions that made sense to you as a youngster became harmful to you later, as you grew up.

EP: Like what?

M: Like doing what other people told you to do, or what

you knew they expected of you, and not doing what you really wanted to do. This may have been in your best interests when you were very young and had to do what your parents said in order to survive, but you never changed the pattern. You hardly ever did what you really wanted to do, and you still don't.

EP: (Heatedly) That's not so! There are times when I do what I want!

M: Not when other people are involved. When others are around, you focus on what you think will please them or on what you think they expect.

EP: What's wrong with that?

M: Nothing, unless it stops you from doing what you really want.

EP: Hmmm.

M: (Softly) It also prevents you from *knowing* what you want.

EP: (Thinking deeply about M's statement) Well, I know what I want right now. I know I don't want things to continue the way they are!

M: That's not knowing what you want. It's knowing what you *don't* want! It's not nearly as useful as knowing what you want.

EP: Oh . . . (Looking surprised) Why is that?

M: Knowing what you *don't* want only tells you what things to eliminate from your life. Knowing what you *want* tells you what to replace them with.

EP: But wouldn't the world be in chaos if everyone did what they really wanted?

M: What makes you say that?

EP: People would probably be running around in the streets robbing, and raping, and pillaging! You just can't let everybody do what they want in life!

M: Where did you learn that?

EP: What do you mean?

M: You learned it somewhere. Someone told it to you.

EP: Why do you say that?

M: Because it isn't true. Earth People often say things like that to stop themselves from doing what they want. They scare themselves. And they try to prevent others from doing what they want, also.

EP: But why wouldn't the world be chaotic?

M: People as a whole wouldn't *want* the world to be in chaos. Chaos gets in the way of success. Given the choice, people would intuitively work out a method to do what they wanted, but in a way that kept the world from becoming chaotic.

EP: (Grudgingly) Well, in a way that makes sense.

M: We've gotten off the track. We were talking about the detrimental decisions you made when you were young. What would you like to discuss now?

EP: Well, right now I'm still hung up on this issue of being able to do what I want. If you want to know the truth, I guess I really don't *know* what I want. Things are so confused.

M: You knew what you wanted when you were young, and you can know it again.

EP: (Looking surprised) Huh? How can you be so sure?

M: Decisions! It's all done with decisions! A long time ago you decided it wasn't in your best interests to know what you wanted—it was more important for you to know what others wanted *of* you. After all, *they* provided your food and shelter. So you gave up thinking about what you wanted, and soon you no longer even *knew* what you wanted. Your decision made sense, then.

EP: How did it make sense?

M: Survival. You did it to survive. However, what you decided once, you can *redecide*. Your survival is no longer at stake.

EP: (Almost disbelieving) Are you saying that in order to survive when I was young, I decided to not even *think* about what I wanted, and since my survival is no longer at stake, I can begin thinking about it once again?

M: Exactly.

EP: Wow! That's a really strange notion. Even the idea that I don't know what I want sounds crazy, when you think of it.

M: Yes, I know.

EP: (Still disbelieving) But to say that I *decided* not to know what I want when I was young—well, that's really hard to believe!

M: It's something few people understand, but it's a valuable awareness. And to know that you can change your early decisions is an important insight. It can bring you great power!

EP: (Enthusiastically) Can you tell me how to go about changing my decisions!

M: (Slowly) There's no way I can tell you how. The decision-making process just happens. It comes naturally to all Earth People.

EP: If you can't tell me how, can you *show* me?

M: No. It's an individual experience which you must learn for yourself. It may not seem possible to you now, because you used the decision-making process itself to stop deciding. In a sense, you decided not to decide. But that doesn't have to be forever.

EP: Let me get this straight, now. You're saying that once I remember how to decide what I want, I'll be able to automatically *get* anything I want?

M: Almost, but not quite. It's not really automatic, and it's not magical. Once you decide you want something, you must then decide if you're willing to do what's necessary in order to get it.

EP: I knew there was a catch somewhere.

M: In a way, yes, but it's not as bad as you think. As you relearn how to decide what you want, you'll find you can get many things much more easily than you ever thought possible.

EP: Really?

M: Yes. Since you gave up deciding what you wanted, you never got much practice *arranging to get* what you wanted. It became hard for you to do—which convinced you even more not to try.

EP: So until I get some practice at it, it'll still be hard for me?

M: Yes. You'll probably have to give up something familiar in order to get what you want, and, in the past, the trade-off seemed too steep a price to pay. There will be times in the future when it still won't seem worth the effort. You'll need to remember that each time you give up something familiar, you'll be getting closer to attaining your goal.

EP: (Hesitantly) What will I have to give up in order to get what I want?

M: Often something from your past: some idea, some relationship, some way of doing things, or some other plan you might have. At the very least, you'll have to give up time—time you might otherwise put to a different use. But aside from time, and whatever legal restrictions society imposes—if they're important to you—there are no external limitations on what you can get.

EP: The sky's the limit?!

M: Yes. The only limitations you will experience are internal limitations you place on yourself, usually by making decisions about what you do and do not want, and what you can and cannot get. It certainly doesn't take great intelligence, or luck, to become either rich or happy. And you could become powerful, too.

EP: (Incredulously) Do you mean that I can become rich, and happy, and powerful, starting from this mess I'm in?

M: Yes. You can if you want to. (Pause) Do you *want* to?

EP: (Speaking very seriously) It all sounds so overwhelming! Now that I think about it, it's hard to say. I guess I really don't know!

M: (Slowly) If you don't know what you want, you can never arrange to get it.

EP: (Pause) (Listening very carefully) What was that?

M: I said that if you don't know what you want, you can never arrange to get it.

EP: That's what I thought you said. That's really a very important statement, isn't it?

M: Yes. You have to learn how you stop yourself from knowing what you want, and then change those decisions from your past that stand in your way.

EP: Is that how successful people do it?

M: Yes. They just don't know how to explain it.

EP: (Long pause) Well, I must admit talking with you has been quite an experience. I'm glad I met you, even if you still claim you're a Martian. Will you be around long?

M: I'll be here as long as you need me.

EP: Good. I'd like to think about this for a while. Can we talk some more a little later?

M: Just look for me. I'll be here.

EP: Okay. So long, then.

M: So long.

Comments

1. People usually don't make changes in their lives (that is, examine and change their life plan) unless things are so bad, and they're feeling so confused, that they're almost compelled to bring themselves up short and say, "Stop! What's happening? What am I doing with my life?" (If this has ever happened to you, you may have a sense of what EP is starting to go through.) People usually won't make any attempt to really change their lives until they're somehow brought to the realization that their present plan has them on a collision course with disaster. This realization is often accompanied by a sinking feeling in the pit of the stomach, and the sensation of walking alone into a long dark tunnel with no light visible at the other end. It's a chilling experience. Often it's followed by moments (or days, or weeks) of extreme confusion, self-doubt, drifting, and depression. During this period a person learns to question and examine all aspects of his life. It's almost as if a separate part of him

suddenly becomes available to stand apart and observe, ask questions, and provide feedback.

One of your goals while reading this book will be to allow yourself to arrive at this point (if you haven't done so already), no matter how uncomfortable it may be. You need to walk into your own tunnel, as it were, and find your own Martian.

2. If you do this, one of the first things you may discover is that you really don't know what you want. You may find you know what you *don't* want (i.e., you don't want your life to continue in its current direction), but you may still have considerable difficulty determining exactly what you *want*.

Conceptualizing what we want is one of the very first skills we learn as children. It comes to us naturally, but instead of encouraging it, so it can blossom, most parents try to squelch it. What *we* want conflicts with what *they* want. We're told that we shouldn't want it, that we don't deserve it, that we're *bad* for wanting it, and that we simply can't have it! Soon, we have every reason in the world to stop wanting it. In the few cases where we're allowed to know what we want, our choices are usually limited and very clearly defined. We may be permitted to decide what we want for Christmas, for instance, or for breakfast, but be given little chance to determine what we want in life itself—where the choices are infinite, but must first be conceptualized before they can be obtained.

The ability to conceptualize what you want is the *single most important factor* in becoming rich and happy. Everyone who becomes successful does it automatically. ("Conceptualize" means seeing all aspects of what you want so clearly that its attainability is apparent at the moment you decide you want it.) As you read this book, it will be helpful for you to count the ways you stop yourself from knowing what you want, and the number of times you find that you simply can't make choices, *even when those choices are presented to you!* You must plan to give yourself permission to want things you never thought you could have, and you must permit yourself to obtain them.

3. As an exercise, examine some of the decisions you've made about how you decide what you want.

(a) What would be an ideal life for you? (What's most important to you: comfort, excitement, security, love, adventure, or power?)

(b) How would you define success? (How high do you set your sights? Do you set them "too " high and never reach them? Do you avoid setting them "too" high because you're not "good enough" to reach them? Do you set them so that with an appropriate effort you *can* reach them?)

(c) Do you wait to see if others (family, friends, or associates) want the same things you do before you start trying to achieve them?

(d) How many of your goals are based on what your mother and father wanted for you?

(e) When in your life did you start wanting all the things that are really important to you? (Your career; the type of person you married or spend time with; the type of home you have; your life style.) What influenced you?

(f) How easy is it for you to conceptualize what you want? What must you learn about it to do it better?

CHAPTER TWO

EP Starts
His Journey

EP: Hi, Martian.

M: Hi.

EP: I've been giving some thought to what you said. I guess one of the reasons I can't say for sure I want to become rich and happy is that it all seems so far away. I mean, it doesn't have anything to do with *my* life! Right now, I'd just like to get out of this mess I'm in.

M: They both involve the same process. You can use the process to get out of your mess, and then you can continue to use it to get anything else you want.

EP: Well, I *do* want to get out of this mess.

M: Good.

EP: But I don't know where to start!

M: *When* is a more useful question to ask yourself.

EP: What do you mean, "when"?

M: *When* you will start is more important than *where* you will start.

EP: Why is that?

M: Looking for a place to start, and never finding it, is a way to keep yourself from starting.

EP: (Looking puzzled) *Keep* myself from starting?

M: Yes. *You're* in charge of whether you start or not, and you're in charge of *when* you start.

EP: How can I decide to start when I don't know what's entailed?

M: When will you start to determine what's entailed?

EP: Oh. I see what you mean. The *when* question again. (Pause) Well . . . (Gritting his teeth) I guess it's now or never.

M: Will you start now?

EP: Yes!

M: Okay, then. Start.

EP: (In a determined voice) All right! What do I need to do?

M: You first need to learn to see and hear like a Martian.

EP: (Incredulously) See and hear like a Martian? What's so important about *that*?

M: Once you see and hear like a Martian, you'll see where you are, what you're doing, and where it's leading you. You'll hear what you're saying, and where your words lead. Then you'll know what to change. Seeing and hearing provide a base from which to start.

EP: Is that why most people never get out of their rut —why they never change? Because they don't have a place to start *from*?

M: Yes. They never see, so they don't know where they are. To get from point A to point B, you must first know where point A is. They never learn where point A is, so they never get to B.

EP: They skip the very first step!

M: Exactly.

EP: Wow! That's absolutely fascinating. (Wondering) But why can you Martians see and hear so much better than Earth People?

M: It's not that we see better. It's that we don't place interpretations on what we see. Earth People see briefly —they see *part* of what's happening—but then they place interpretations on what they see and stop themselves from seeing any further.

EP: (Looking puzzled) I don't understand.

M: Yesterday your boss frowned at you—or, at least, you *thought* he frowned at you. You became worried because you thought he was angry with you. You worried all afternoon. Actually, all you saw was a frown. You made assumptions about the frown, and let these assumptions influence you for the rest of the day. (Looking serious) You do things like that all the time. You confuse your interpretation of events with the events themselves. You don't *see,* and leave it at that. Actually, your boss frowned because he had a headache and he had more work than he could handle. It had nothing at all to do with *you.*

EP: How do you know that?

M: I've observed him before and can recognize when he's in pain.

EP: I guess I never thought of it that way before. (Looking bothered) Can you give me another example?

M: All right. Tell me what happened at lunch today.

EP: Lunch? I ate a sandwich. What's there to tell?

M: And before eating?

EP: Oh. (Pause) Now I remember! I asked my friend Mary to go to lunch with me. She didn't want to, and I felt really bad for a while. I wondered what I'd done wrong.

M: What was your assumption?

EP: Assumption? (Pause) Oh. You mean the assumption I'd done something wrong?

M: Yes. See what I mean? You heard Mary's words and assumed that you'd done something wrong. You didn't just *hear,* you interpreted. Actually, all Mary wanted was to have some time to herself.

EP: I think I'm beginning to catch on! Do you have other examples?

M: Sure. You often assume people are talking about you when they're really making statements about themselves.

EP: I do? When do I do that?

M: Every time someone you're talking to uses the word "you."

EP: I don't quite follow. (Pause) You're saying that when

I'm talking to someone and he uses the word "you," he might not be referring to *me?*

M: Yes. You're making an assumption based solely on some of the words he used. You're not just *hearing*.

EP: But what am I not hearing?

M: That he's usually not talking about you. He's usually talking about himself.

EP: Wait a minute! This is crazy! (Acting flustered) Could you give me any examples?

M: Sure. When your boss told you last week that he thought you'd done a good job, you felt pleased. You thought he was talking about you.

EP: Well he *was!*

M: No. He was talking about himself. He was saying *he* felt pleased.

EP: But he didn't *say* that! He said that *I'd* done a good job. He referred directly to *me!*

M: That's what I mean. You insist on making assumptions.

EP: Didn't he say that? Didn't he use those words?

M: He *did* use those words, but what he was doing was making a statement about himself. He was saying what *he* felt, and what *he* thought.

EP: (Pause) Oh. I think I see what you mean. But doesn't *everybody* do that? Doesn't everybody just say what he thinks and feels?

M: Yes. And that's exactly my point. If you weren't so concerned with your own self-importance, and so hypnotized by the word "you," you'd always hear things exactly as they are.

EP: Hypnotized?

M: Yes. Now, when you hear the word "you," you believe it has something to do with you personally, and you gauge your responses accordingly.

EP: And what would I hear if I weren't hypnotized?

M: Someone making a statement that included the word "you."

EP: I don't . . . (Gulp) Oh! You mean I wouldn't feel complimented, or in other cases disappointed or de-

pressed, because of what he said. I'd be hearing him
objectively!

M: Right.

EP: (Thinking deeply) And how will this help me get out
of the mess I'm in?

M: You'll be able to devote much more time and energy
to getting out of your mess because you won't be tied up in
responding to the hypnotic effect of others.

EP: Hmmm. I think I see what you mean. I really spend a
lot of time doing that. (Pausing thoughtfully) Is there anything else I'll need to learn in order to see and hear clearly?

M: Yes. You'll need to learn to see and hear with a
broader perspective. Are you interested?

EP: I sure am!

M: All right, then. You'll need to learn to detach yourself
from your surroundings, and to see yourself as a disinterested observer; as if you were *me,* seeing you. If you'd done
this with your boss, or today at lunch with Mary, you'd have
seen yourself *reacting* to them and you'd have been able to
stop yourself from reacting as you did.

EP: But what would I have done instead?

M: (Patiently) Now you're talking about *doing.* That involves a different decision from *seeing,* and we haven't even
determined, for sure, that you want to *see!*

EP: What do you mean?

M: It's no help to take decisions out of sequence. *Seeing*
comes first. After we're certain you've decided to *see,* then
we can talk about *doing.*

EP: All right. Can you teach me how to see and hear like a
Martian?

M: No. It isn't teachable. But you can learn by watching
and listening to me.

EP: That doesn't seem too hard.

M: Well, the watching and listening may not be difficult,
but the decision to see and hear like a Martian *can* be. It's a
different decision from deciding to just watch and listen. In
fact, it's a decision you may not want to make. You may have
to give up your fantasies.

EP: Huh?

M: You have certain ideas about life that aren't consistent with the way life really is. These ideas are fantasies that you adopted in the past, which have served you until now, and you may not want to give them up.

EP: I remember you said I might have to give up something familiar to get what I want. Is this what you meant? Were you referring to my fantasies?

M: Fantasies are one example, but you'll also have to give up other things.

EP: Like what?

M: You'll know them when they appear. It always happens this way. You'll learn about them when the time is right.

EP: What sort of fantasies will I have to give up?

M: Your fantasies about life that stop you from seeing clearly.

EP: You mean about the way I want life to be?

M: And about people, and the way you've seen them in the past. You've seen them not as they are, but rather as you wished they were. You'll also have to give up your fantasies about how to do things in life—all those ways of doing things which in the past you thought, or hoped, would work, but which in fact never did. Once you see your old fantasies for what they are, and once you know they will never work, you'll be able to operate much more effectively. But many people prefer to hold on to their old ways, even if they are fantasies that will never bring success.

EP: Martian?

M: Yes.

EP: I'm sad.

M: Oh. What about?

EP: I know so many people like that—people who don't want to give up their fantasies. My own father was like that. And my mother, too, to some extent. My father kept thinking the world was fair, and people were honest. He'd look at someone and believe that person was honest, whether he was or not. My father believed if he just worked hard, and stayed out of trouble, everything would work out all right.

Well, it didn't! And he could never understand why.

M: Many people build their lives on fantasies.

EP: So many of my friends do it. They hope and they dream, and the world just doesn't fit their hopes and dreams. But *I* hope and dream, so there must be a lot of the world that I miss seeing, also. Is it like that for me, too, Martian?

M: Yes. In many ways. There are many fantasies you need to reexamine. Each will involve a separate decision. At each moment of clarity you'll choose one of two paths: either to return to your old fantasies, or to push forward toward greater clarity by giving those fantasies up. If you choose to move toward clarity, you'll arrive at a new level of awareness and your life will change.

EP: But won't I become cold and calculating after giving up my fantasies?

M: No. People always think this will happen, but it never does. You'll merely replace your old fantasies with new ones—but not until after you have learned to see.

EP: I hope so. It's a little scary. (Pause) Well, let's see what I've learned so far. First, when I learn to see and hear like a Martian I'll no longer make assumptions about events, nor place instant interpretations on them. I'll see them only as they occur, without adding a bias of my own. I'll also have a broader perspective. And I'll be able to look at myself objectively, from outside myself, as if I were you, seeing me. I'll see myself doing whatever I'm doing. (Feeling self-satisfied) Now, is there anything else I'll be able to do?

M: Yes. The first type of seeing you mentioned involves learning to see the external world; that is, people and events around you. The second involves learning to see yourself *in* the external world; that is, stepping outside yourself, as if you were a third-party observer, collecting data on both you and your surroundings. But there's still one more type of seeing to learn.

EP: A third type?

M: Yes, Even more subtle than the first two. It involves learning to see *inside* yourself; that is, learning to know what you're experiencing with your thoughts and feelings. In particular, it involves learning to hear what you're saying to yourself, and learning to know what you're feeling.

EP: Oh. You mean that *feelings* are also information to be collected; that feelings are data, just like everything else?

M: Yes.

EP: But, Martian, there are lots of times when I don't feel anything at all.

M: Oh, really?

EP: Yes.

M: What are you feeling right now?

EP: Nothing!

M: Then tell me about your flushed face.

EP: . . .

M: Well?

EP: Darn it. I don't like you reading my mind!

M: And what are you feeling?

EP: I guess I'm shocked. You caught me by surprise.

M: You guess?

EP: Actually, I felt you were invading my privacy; you got too close to home. (Pause) Scared! Yeah, I felt scared.

M: You sure don't like to acknowledge what you feel, do you?

EP: No . . . (Thinking a moment) Tell me, are most people like this or am I just a bit peculiar?

M: Most people are the same way. All Earth People constantly feel something. It's part of their mechanism. Even if they're just feeling numb, or deadened, and don't *think* they're feeling anything, they're actually feeling numb and deadened.

EP: But how could you tell what *I* was feeling just now?

M: You wouldn't have started this conversation if you weren't feeling some doubt, some wonderment, or possibly some curiosity about this process of seeing like a Martian. These are the sorts of things Earth People feel in such situations. And as soon as I said you were feeling something, you started feeling embarrassed, or scared.

EP: Did you know I was feeling scared before I told you?

M; Yes.

EP: How could you tell?

M: By *seeing*. I observed what happened to your face.

EP: Why is it so important for me to know what I feel?

M: Ah! That's a very interesting question. It's one I myself asked when I first came to Earth. It happens that Earth People have a very peculiar mechanism that motivates them to say and do things mainly on the basis of what they feel. Yet, interestingly, very few Earth People actually *know* what they feel. And many of those who do have trouble acknowledging it.

EP: Why is that?

M: It's a very strange phenomenon. It appears that most young Earth People are *trained* by their mothers and fathers not to know what they feel.

EP: That's hard to believe. Why do you say that?

M: Well, Earth People, as a group, have never developed an effective way of dealing with their feelings—particularly their bad feelings like anger and guilt, but also some of their good feelings, like love and joy and sexuality. They're trained not to feel these feelings, or not to feel them too intensely; or if they *do* feel them, they're trained not to be aware of them. Only a very few lucky children escape this difficulty.

EP: Why do you say they're lucky?

M: Because they grow up with a great advantage over everyone else. They develop unusually fine instincts and intuition. Their "gut" responses to life are highly accurate, and their perceptions are unusually well developed. They acquire a good "feel" for life, and a talent for doing many things. They become very successful.

EP: All because they learned to know what they feel? Don't brains and intelligence have anything to do with it?

M: Not very much. Not nearly as much as people think.

EP: You mean that everyone who learns to know what he feels becomes successful?

M: Not necessarily. But he always has the potential. It depends on what decisions he makes about using this potential.

EP: So, what you're saying is that it's more important for me to learn what I feel than it is to learn anything else?

M: Yes. Particularly at this point in your life. You need to redevelop your potential. Information about other things may be useful later on.

EP: That sounds pretty silly. I'm not a basket case. I already know what I feel—at least most of the time.

M: You know *that* you feel, but you frequently don't know *what* you feel; and you don't know how to act on your feelings. Often the fact that you're feeling something is only a dim awareness in the back of your mind. You're not close enough to your feelings to know what they are, and you don't know how to operate from them.

EP: Hmmm. But why do mothers and fathers train their children not to know what they feel if it's so harmful?

M: They don't know any better. They themselves were trained that way. It's been passed down from generation to generation. They do it without thinking. It's been going on like that for a long time.

EP: Is this training done consciously?

M: Not at all. Sometimes it isn't even done actively. Sometimes a youngster's environment is made so uncomfortable for him that he trains *himself* not to feel, or not to know what he feels. He splits himself off from his feelings.

EP: (Taking a deep breath) I hear what you're saying about all this, and I think I might be this type of person. I might have a lot of feelings I simply don't *want* to feel. I mean, there's no sense dwelling on the fact that I'm depressed if I can't do anything about it.

M: Ah, but you *can* do something about it. You can change your feelings. It's just that most Earth People don't know they can.

EP: You mean that I can stop feeling depressed, and feel happy instead? And I can get rid of my feelings of self-doubt, and actually feel self-confident and happy, all the time?!

M: Absolutely! And when you feel self-confident, you'll be able to accomplish a great deal more than ever before. The tradeoffs you'll need to make will be easier, too. In fact, you'll be able to get just about anything you want—and with a great deal of satisfaction.

EP: And can you teach me to do this?

M: There you go again! Thinking someone else must teach you and denying your capacity to learn for yourself!

EP: I don't understand.

M: I know. But it's something I can't teach you. You must learn it for yourself. It's an individual experience.

EP: (Hesitating) But do you think I *can*?

M: You're doubting yourself. You were trained to doubt yourself. You'll have to learn not to do that, and you'll have to give up the feeling of self-doubt that induces such questions.

EP: But is there anything you can do to help me?

M: Yes there is. The process of getting clear is like a journey, and I can travel alongside you as you go through it.

EP: Will you help direct me?

M: No. No one can direct your journey. It wouldn't be *yours* if they could. But you'll be making a series of decisions along the way, and I can help you outline your options. I can also remind you of earlier decisions you've made that may reflect on your new ones.

EP: (Pause) How will I know when the process is finished—when my journey is complete?

M: You'll know.

EP: Could you give me a clue?

M: When the process is complete, you'll have the clarity of a Martian and be able to get anything you want.

EP: (Smiling) Boy! That's exciting!! We'll have lots to talk about then, won't we?

M: No. At the end of your journey you won't need to see me anymore. I'll just disappear.

EP: You'll disappear? (Pause) I don't want you to disappear.

M: We'll have nothing more to talk about. My observations will have become a part of you. All along your journey you'll be asking questions of me, but at the end you will have nothing left to ask. You won't miss me. You'll be your own person. You'll experience a sense of completeness, and my departure will seem a natural conclusion to our relationship.

EP: Wow! That's really hard to conceive!

M: I know. Are you ready to start?

EP: Yes. I am.

M: Good. Let's rest a little. Tomorrow we'll begin.

Comments

1. This chapter has lots of meat in it. It's worth reading many times over. First, there's the question of "when." If you're interested in changing your life, "when" is the only relevant question to ask yourself. Asking "what to do" or "where to start"—or answering "I don't know" to *any* question you might ask yourself—will only prevent you from starting your new life.

2. People who become rich and happy "see" things differently from other people. This isn't a special skill they're born with, but rather an ability everyone has. Most people lose touch with this ability, however, as they grow up and learn to "understand" what people "mean." (Learning to understand includes learning to interpret, to make assumptions, and to draw conclusions.) They begin substituting what they've *learned* for what they might otherwise *perceive*. People who become successful somehow avoid this. They hold onto their ability to see while *supplementing* it with their interpretations. Their interpretations, and assumptions, are never absolute. (They never fully "understand," in the sense that they stop from seeing further.)

To recapture this skill, you must learn to question all your automatic, unthinking assumptions about life as you know it. You must rethink all your previous conclusions. You must allow yourself to see things without trying to understand them, and when you think you understand them, you must avoid simple conclusions so you can continue to see.

3. This book is filled with examples of assumptions EP has made about himself, about the people around him, and about the way the world operates. Many are based on information he's learned, and many are pure fantasy. Just as in real life, most of these assumptions are not clearly labeled as such. It's up to you to discover them for yourself. The more sensible or logical they seem, the more harmful they may be.

4. Seeing where you are, so you know what to change *from,* is absolutely essential to altering the course of your life. Many people are "afraid" to "look at themselves." They decide at some point in their lives that they're not going to like what they see, so they stop themselves from seeing it. When you find yourself doing this, you'll need to consider reexamining this decision. It's perhaps the most dysfunctional decision you've ever made. You simply can't hide from yourself and get rich.

5. The three types of seeing covered in this chapter —seeing the external world, seeing yourself *in* the external world, and seeing within yourself—come easily to most successful people. Thus they get a much better idea of how to operate, and a much better sense of what they really want to get out of life, than the average person. *Seeing* is indispensable to getting what you want! (As someone once said, "How can you ever get what you want if you can't even see it in the first place?")

6. The idea that people are motivated to do things on the basis of what they *feel* is such an obvious notion to some people as to barely merit mentioning. To many others who don't *know* what they feel, it's simply mind-boggling. They've been taught to do things on the basis of what they *think.* They've cut themselves off from their feelings for a wide variety of reasons. Many men are taught to be strong

(to acknowledge they *feel* is a sign of weakness). Many women are taught that some feelings are downright sinful (feeling powerful and feeling sexy, for example). The list of things some people aren't permitted to feel is endless (strong, weak, angry, sad, disappointed, frustrated, and so on).

Those who operate from a life plan leading directly to riches and happiness rarely receive such programming, and if they *do* receive it, they don't buy it. They may think about things before acting, but their final decisions are always based on what they feel. Since they haven't cut themselves off from their feelings (decided *not* to feel), their final decisions are almost always based on an intuitive sense that virtually guarantees success.

7. The notion that people can change what they feel in a given situation (and feel good instead of feeling bad) is counter to the teaching of most of our society. Yet people who become rich and happy *learn to feel good!* They rarely engage in feeling guilty, depressed, or scared, or anything else that drains their mental and emotional energy. Their total attention is fixed on positive goals. They achieve this state, not by hiding from the negative issues in their lives, but by resolving and eliminating such issues. Most of this book is devoted to methods that can help you do the same in your own life.

CHAPTER THREE

EP Sharpens His Perceptions

EP: (Enthusiastically) Okay. I'm ready to start learning to see like a Martian. I really don't have much choice, because I sure don't like this mess I'm in.

M: You can *choose* to keep things the same—to stay in the mess.

EP: (With conviction) That's not an option I'm willing to consider.

M: Good. You sound like you've decided to proceed.

EP: (Pause) You seem convinced that I meant what I said just now—about being ready to start. But how can you tell? How do you know I'm not still just toying with the idea?

M: How did *you* know I was convinced that you were ready?

EP: (Thinking) You sounded convinced.

M: Well, *you* sounded ready to start. If you hadn't been ready, your voice would have been different. It would have been less believable. There would have been some doubt in it. (Pause) Now, you tell *me*. How could *you* tell that I sounded convinced?

EP: I don't know. You just—you just sounded that way.

M: Can you tell the difference between when someone sounds convinced and when he doesn't?

EP: Yes.

M: Do you trust your judgment on this?

EP: Yes.

M: Good! Be sure to remember this conversation. We'll come across situations where you won't trust your perceptions, where you won't believe you can perceive accurately. It will be important for you to remember that you do have this capacity.

EP: (Brightly) Oh . . . I get it! When I trust my perceptions, I'm already seeing like a Martian. I *can* do it, already—at least sometimes. And if I can do it sometimes, I can do it all the time. I just need to use this skill in more situations.

M: Right.

EP: (Earnestly) But what about people who are lying —people who are trying to fool me? Will I be able to see through *them?*

M: I hear you wanting to make a statement.

EP: Huh?

M: You phrased your sentence as a question, but I heard you wanting to make a statement.

EP: What kind of statement?

M: A statement about how some people can fool you.

EP: No. I wasn't trying to make a statement. I wanted to learn more about people who lie.

M: (Impatiently) Look. I trust my perceptions. I *know* you wanted to make a statement.

EP: (Dumbfounded)

M: Well?

EP: (Grudgingly) Oh, all right, if you insist. People sure can fool me, if they want to. Sometimes I just can't tell if they're lying or not.

M: Good! That's clear.

EP: (Quizzically) How could you tell I really wanted to make a statement when I asked that question?

M: My perceptions. I always trust them.

EP: Then why can't I trust *my* perceptions? How do people fool me?

M: Perceptions happen in the present. *Fooling* happens in the future based on your assumptions and expectations of what's going to happen.

EP: (Brightly) You mean if I don't make assumptions, and if I don't have expectations about the future, then no one can fool me?

M: That's right. You'll be seeing and hearing like a Martian. (Pause) But it may be useful to examine how people fooled you in the past. Can you give me any examples?

EP: Yes. People usually fooled me when they said they were going to do something—and I believed them—and then they went and did something else.

M: Do you hear the assumption in your statement?

EP: Not that I . . . (Pause) You mean the assumption that they'd do what they said they'd do?

M: Yes.

EP: Hmmm. But how can I operate without making assumptions? I have to believe in *somebody!*

M: It's not a matter of believing or not believing. It's a matter of *seeing*.

EP: I don't understand.

M: People don't fool you. You fool yourself. You fool yourself with your expectations.

EP: How?

M: You stop yourself from seeing.

EP: (Incredulously) Do you mean to say I shouldn't believe anybody?

M: I didn't say that. You're not hearing me clearly.

EP: But there has to be someone in the world I can trust!

M: You'll fool yourself as long as you continue to have assumptions and expectations.

EP: That sounds so cold and calculating—like you're saying never to trust anyone.

M: I'm not speaking of trust. I'm speaking of *seeing*. You can see only in the present. If you're dealing with the future, you're either guessing what will happen, or you're believing something will happen, which is just another form of guessing. If you're *believing* things about the future, you'll stop yourself from seeing, and you won't be prepared for changes in people's behavior. You'll be surprised, shocked, or hurt when such changes occur.

EP: But what would *you* do if someone lied to you?

M: I'd see him in the present, and I'd hear him speaking about his future actions. As time passed, I'd see that his actions didn't fit his earlier statements. This would have been one of the options I'd considered, although I may have assigned it a low probability. However, it wouldn't disturb me.

EP: You mean, if it were you, he wouldn't have fooled you.

M: I wouldn't have fooled *myself!* As I've said already, I make no assumptions. I'm not concerned about whether or not people do as they say. I have no personal stake in their future actions.

EP: But sometimes I *have* to depend on other people.

M: I know.

EP: So what do you suggest?

M: If you have to guess about their future actions, then guess. If you get good at guessing, you'll learn to figure the odds well, and you won't be wrong very often. But remember, a guess is only a guess. Don't confuse a guess with a guarantee.

EP: You mean no one can predict the future?

M: That's right. You can *see* only in the present. It's a fantasy to believe you can see into the future.

EP: I never thought of it that way.

M: This may be one of the fantasies you'll have to give up.

EP: I think you're right. It sounds as if it makes sense. But what actually *is* my fantasy?

M: That you can predict the future.

EP: (Pause) This all ties together, doesn't it? As soon as I decide someone's honest, and I can *believe* him, I stop myself from watching him any further. I stop myself from seeing. I believe I can predict the future on the basis of what he's said and how he's said it. But no one can really predict the future. By clinging to this fantasy, I stop myself from being prepared for times when people don't live up to my expectations. I fool myself. It isn't that the other person lies—or maybe he *does* lie, but it doesn't make any difference. The main thing is that I stop myself from seeing!

M: You've got it.

Comments

1. If you want to achieve wealth and happiness, you must be able to trust your perceptions. (You must feel confident that you can *act* on the basis of what you perceive.) To do this, you must be open to receive all the information available to you, and you must be able to see the consistency, or lack of consistency, in what you observe.

To deal effectively with the world at large, you need to know whether or not people will do what their words and actions say they'll do. You must be able to tell if their tone of voice fits their words; if the look in their eyes fits the sound of their voice; if their faces say the same thing their bodies say. Discrepancies or inconsistencies between body, voice, eyes, face, words, and general attitude can be a signal that people are about to fool you, or at the very least fool themselves. (They're probably not aware of the discrepancies, and may not even know they're planning something other than what they're saying.)

Most of us, in growing up, decide to receive only *some* of the information available to us. We ignore the rest. We bypass many important clues that would help us determine with much greater accuracy what's really going on around us. Our early decisions to operate from limited data are among the easiest for us to redecide. Most people don't like to be fooled, and certainly don't like to arrange things so that they fool *themselves*. If you find this is true for yourself, you might consider checking out your perceptions with someone else, just as EP does with M at the beginning of this chapter.

2. The notion that questions may really be statements

about the people asking them may sound strange, but the next time *you* ask a question, listen to yourself. You may find that what you're really saying is, "I already know the answer but I'm afraid to admit it," or, "I want to trap this guy because he's making me uncomfortable," or "I want to stay confused, and I'll do so by asking this complicated question." The purpose in listening for the statement is to find out where you really are. As soon as you start listening for the statements in other people's questions (look for the *reasons* they're asking the questions), you'll be able to respond directly to the statement rather than be sidetracked by the camouflage.

3. You might conclude from this chapter that I'm suggesting you shouldn't trust people. I'm not! The issue isn't one of trusting others, but rather of learning to trust *your own perceptions of others*. Most people won't lie, or deliberately try to manipulate you. They're more likely to operate in good faith, but with conflicting interests and either incomplete or distorted information. Your job is to see the incompleteness, the confusions, and the discrepancies. Once you do, people will no longer seem untrustworthy, tricky, or undependable. They'll merely seem unclear, uncertain, or confused. You'll experience no need to act defensively or to protect yourself from them. A great deal of your energy will be freed to get on with getting what you want.

CHAPTER FOUR

EP Learns
to See from
Outside Himself

EP: I've been thinking about when you told me—that one way to see like a Martian is to step outside myself and see myself as if I were a disinterested observer. I really don't understand how that can be done.

M: Ah! It involves seeing yourself *in* the world—you and the world around you, simultaneously.

EP: Huh?

M: Well, what's happening right now?

EP: What do you mean?

M: How would you describe what's happening between us right at this moment?

EP: (Looking doubtful) I don't know . . .

M: Okay. Let me show you. Just now you said you'd been thinking about seeing yourself from outside yourself—you said you didn't understand how it could be done. I responded by asking you how you would describe what was happening right now.

EP: Uh-huh.

M: Then you asked me what I meant. I repeated my question in a different way. I asked you to describe what was

happening between us, to which you responded, "I don't
know." Then I started demonstrating how to do it, which
I'm doing now, and now I'm stopping, and at the same time,
describing the fact that I'm stopping. See? That's how you
do it.

EP: Oh!

M: Now *you* do it. It should be easy.

EP: (Looking slightly scared) What do you mean?

M: Well, you just saw how I did it, so I'm suggesting that
you give it a try.

EP: Hmmm. (Hesitating) That all went by pretty fast.
Could you do it again?

M: Sure. When I asked you to try, to see if you could do it,
you chose not to try, but rather to ask me to show you again.
You said the first time I went too fast. So, now I'm showing
you again. Since you look somewhat puzzled, I have a
hunch you'll either do it for yourself, right now, or you will
give up.

EP: Well . . . (Frowning and looking puzzled)

M: In addition, I sense that as I continue to talk, you're
beginning to build up frustration within yourself, and you
may not feel comfortable asking me to show you many more
times. In fact, if you don't decide to do it now, you probably
won't get around to trying it again for quite a while.

EP: (His voice exhilarated and his eyes sparkling) Now I
see it!!! . . . Wow! I was just about to say I didn't understand! I was about to back off, until you said I might do just
that. Then all of a sudden I *did* understand! But it wasn't
because of your words. I was watching you as you demon-
strated, and I suddenly saw you were describing what was
going on between us—at the *very moment* it was going on.
The description of the event had become the event itself!
This awareness hit me all of a sudden, just after you saw me
building up frustration within myself. And now, as you
listen, I'm telling you how I had this insight. (Pause) Hey!!
I'm doing it right now! I'm speaking, and describing what
I'm saying at the same time! I'm seeing myself from outside

myself, and I'm telling you what I'm seeing!

M: Very good.

EP: Wow! That's really great! (Pause) The only thing I can't figure out is how you got me to do it.

M: There's a trick. If you just tried to focus on seeing, you'd probably never see. Most people never do. So I asked you, instead, to focus on *describing*—describing what was going on between us. When your mind was intent on describing, and not seeing, you learned to see, automatically. That's because it's impossible to describe something without seeing it.

EP: So in the future, when I want to see, I merely need to start describing things to myself.

M: Exactly. And remember always to include a description of what has occurred in the immediate past, and your hunch as to what might occur in the immediate future.

EP: I see! That's how you actually got me to start describing *our* conversation. I remember you said you didn't think I'd feel comfortable asking you to demonstrate many more times. As I thought about it, I knew you were right. I kind of decided that it was now or never.

M: And then you *did* it!

EP: Yes. I did. I wonder why . . .

M: There were only two choices you could make. You could either try it, or not try it. I merely made your options clearer for you by stating them. If you'd chosen not to try, it would have been contrary to your earlier decision to see like a Martian. You knew this, and at some level it was more important to you to stick with your earlier decision. I'm glad you took the risk.

EP: Yeah. Me too. I can already see myself using this later on. In the middle of an argument I'll be able to describe to myself what I'm doing, and I'll be able to figure out how the argument might end. Then I'll be able to just change the ending, or even stop the argument in midstream. I can think of a half a dozen other uses as well. I'm really going to get a lot out of being able to see myself from outside myself!

Comments

1. You now have a way to examine whatever you're doing at any point in time—a way to see yourself in the world so you can decide whether being where you are, doing what you're doing, or talking to whomever you're talking to is what you really *want* to be doing. Once you can see where you are, you can decide whether being there is helping you forward your new goals, and if it isn't, you can simply change it.

2. Contrary to what we've been conditioned to believe from childhood, learning isn't always just collecting facts. From the very first moment we start learning, our parents and teachers ask us questions about what we *know*, what *facts* we've learned, and what we *think!* Even when we're asked how we feel, the question usually means "What are you thinking?" Although we're taught that *experience* is the best teacher, we're usually robbed of the opportunity to develop our own experiential learning skills.

   This is the first chapter to present something that can be learned only by experiencing it. You can't be told how to see, but you may have begun to sense and experience something of the process for yourself. If you haven't, or if this chapter didn't make much sense to you (or if it seemed extraneous or uninteresting), don't worry about it. Subsequent chapters will approach the issue differently. You might want to wait a while and come back to give Chapter 4 another try.

3. If the subject matter *did* strike you as valuable, you might have noted how M frustrated EP to the point where he energized himself to actually see from outside himself. It's very much like learning to swim, or dive, or ride a bike. There comes a time when you either do it or you don't. M got EP to recognize that he was rapidly reaching this "now or never" point, and would need to make his decision shortly.

4. One of the factors that distinguishes a successful life

plan, or life script, from an unsuccessful one is the decision a person makes to arrange his or her life to confront these "now or never" points all along the way. It's the key to experiential learning! To succeed, you will not only need to arrange your life to confront these points frequently, but you'll also need to decide in favor of "now" rather than "never" almost all the time—and become *comfortable* with the process!

CHAPTER FIVE

EP Gains Greater Perspective

EP: Martian?

M: Yes.

EP: How am I ever going to remember all these things I've been learning lately?

M: Would you be willing to turn your question into a statement?

EP: Oh. That again. How do you know I want to make a statement?

M: I *hear* you wanting to make a statement. Since I trust my perceptions, I know, with absolute certainty, that you want to make a statement. Whether you make it or not is up to you.

EP: What kind of statement?

M: A statement about yourself, and about how you have trouble remembering the things we've been talking about.

EP: (Irritated) Oh. All right. I'm willing to make a statement like that. But will you tell me what this is all about? I still don't understand why I ask you a question when I really want to make a statement.

M: People like to keep things from themselves. They only assume responsibility for acting on information that they admit to themselves they possess.

56

EP: But why would anyone want to do that?

M: Would you make the statement you just said you'd make—the one about remembering all these things you've been learning?

EP: Well, it's hard for me to put into words, but *seeing* isn't quite as easy as I expected.

M: That's not a statement about remembering.

EP: Oh. (Pause) I've been having some trouble remembering to see, especially when I need to do it most. Like in the middle of an argument—when I thought I'd be able to see what I was doing, and then be able to change the future course of the argument. . . . Well, I can't. In fact, I don't even *think* about seeing until after the argument is over.

M: So. The statement is . . . ?

EP: I can't remember to see, especially when I really need to!

M: Now, that's the kind of statement I spoke about when I said people like to keep things from themselves. See how hard it was to get you to say that?

EP: Yeah. (With wonderment) I sure kept trying to avoid it.

M: Do you know what the avoidance was about?

EP: (Flustered) Well, it's embarrassing to admit that you can't remember something when you need to.

M: Is it that part of you doesn't remember and another part of you feels embarrassed when it finds that out?

EP: Sort of . . . (Defensively) What is this? Are you saying I've got a split personality or something?

M: In a sense. But it's not unusual. All Earth People are comprised of separate parts. Each part may either agree or disagree with each of the other parts, and each part may have information the others don't want to hear.

EP: Boy. You're really pushing me. You're asking me to believe a lot.

M: I'm not asking you to believe. I'm speaking of my observations. You can observe this, too.

EP: (Incredulously) You mean if *I* really looked at people, I'd see them comprised of separate parts?

M: Absolutely.

EP: Well, I'll really have to think that one over. But before we go any further, would you do me a favor? I'm still bothered by this stuff about making statements instead of asking questions.

M: Okay. What's bothering you?

EP: Well, I started this conversation—back at the beginning—by asking you how I could remember all these things I've been learning. I really need something to help me remember. Now it seems to me that asking you that sort of question is a better way of getting help than making any sort of statement! *Statements* don't obtain help!

M: When you said, "How am I going to remember all these things I've been learning?" I *heard* you wanting to make a statement about having trouble remembering. If you *also* wanted to ask me for a method to help you remember, you were saying two separate things. The way to do that is to make the statement and then ask the question, rather than ask me just one question that avoids the statement and keeps me in the dark about your real need for help.

EP: (Grudgingly) Okay. You win. I guess it wouldn't hurt to make a statement and then ask the question.

M: No! Don't feel grudging about it! It's more important than you've acknowledged. It's actually *better* to do both. It helps you *hear* yourself, and it helps you to stop hiding information from yourself.

EP: (Still grudgingly) Well, all right. If you say so.

M: I hear you saying that you agree with me, but my perceptions tell me that you really don't. You don't have to agree with me. It is not an issue of agreement or disagreement. You also don't have to turn your questions into statements if you don't want to.

EP: Well, if that's the case, why have you kept insisting that I do just that?!

M: I haven't insisted. Each time you've asked a question that was really a statement, I've told you what I heard. I've told you of my perceptions. I am willing *not* to tell you of my perceptions, if you prefer.

EP: No. I certainly don't want that. Then I'd have no way of ever learning to see and hear like a Martian! But it's still a dilemma for me. If I agree to continue to hear your perceptions, then I have to be prepared to listen to you tell me that I'm secretive, that I keep information from myself.

M: Yes. You'll also have to give up your fantasy about *not* keeping information from yourself. This is one of those moments of clarity I spoke of earlier.

EP: But who are you to say it's a *fantasy?!*

M: You seem angry.

EP: You didn't answer my question!

M: I'm telling you my perception.

EP: What? That I'm angry?

M: Yes. Were you aware of it?

EP: (Heatedly) Of course I was aware of it! What do you think I am? Stupid?

M: You did not appear to be aware of it. You do not *now* appear to be aware of it.

EP: (Calming down) Hmmm. All right. I see what you mean. I was getting carried away with myself.

M: What was the anger about?

EP: I don't know.

M: Yes, you do. Tell me.

EP: Boy! You're really pushy today. I was angry because you think I *keep* things from myself!

M: So why get angry?

EP: Because I *don't* keep things from myself.

M: That doesn't fit with my perception.

EP: Who are you to say what fits or not? Just who do you think you are?!

M: You're angry again. What do you want of me?

EP: I want you to say that I don't keep things from myself!

M: That doesn't fit with my perception. I have no reason to say something that is different from what I perceive.

EP: Who says your perceptions are the right ones?

M: You're still angry.

EP: (Reflecting) So I am. . . . What's going on, anyway?

M: You're at a moment of clarity, as I said before. Your anger is directed at having to make a choice between clarity and fantasy.

EP: I don't have to make a choice if I don't want to!

M: No, you don't. But if you don't choose to see clearly, I'll disappear.

EP: What do you mean?

M: I have no interest in supporting your fantasies. I know what I see and hear. They are *my* perceptions. Your conversation about them, right now, is not relevant to me.

EP: I don't want you to disappear.

M: Then you must make a choice. Staying stuck is not helpful. You must either go forward with me and become clearer, or go backward by yourself to your old fantasies. If you go backward and return to your fantasies, I'll disappear. It won't pose a problem for you, however, because from that point on you'll be able to think of *me* as a fantasy. I won't be a threat to you. This is a moment of clarity—the choice is yours.

EP: (Pause) But if you leave me, I won't ever to able to learn to see like a Martian—and I won't be able to change my life.

M: Correct. But that's not a problem for most Earth People. They often choose to stay stuck, or to move backward.

EP: (Emphatically) Well, not *me!*

M: Oh?

EP: Yeah. I've got to learn to see! Going back is too miserable.

M: Okay, then. Tell me about these different parts of yourself, and how one part keeps information from the other.

EP: Well, I've never thought of myself as having separate parts. I've always thought of myself more as having just one part that changed a lot. Like, one moment I'd feel relaxed and comfortable, and the next, tense and irritable.

M: That's very perceptive, but not entirely accurate. It's a matter of focus. You've been focusing on yourself as a totality. If you were to focus instead on your separate parts, you'd experience that you in fact didn't change, but merely alternated your separate parts.

EP: How's that?

M: You're comprised of separate parts. *You* don't change, and your parts don't change—at least not very much. Your parts merely take turns surfacing. They appear, and then they disappear. Then they reappear all over again. Each part is different enough from the others so that together, as they come and go, they give the appearance that you're constantly changing. You're really not.

EP: But what is this about focusing?

M: If you focus on yourself as a totality, you'll appear to be changing as each of your parts takes turns emerging. This is how you've seen yourself in the past. But if you focus instead on your separate parts, you'll see that you really remain constant, merely alternating parts.

EP: So in the past when I thought I was changing, I really wasn't. I was just switching parts?

M: That's almost right. Actually, different parts of you were assuming control of your actions at different times.

EP: Does that mean that these parts don't operate simultaneously?

M: Right. They're usually activated one at a time. When one is operating, the others are usually dormant. For example, look at this conversation we've been having. Not long ago you were angry, denying that you had separate parts, ready to fall back on your fantasies. In fact, you probably *would* have returned to your fantasies if I hadn't told you that I'd disappear. Then you underwent a switch. You mentioned that you were aware of changes that seemed to occur in you, like when you changed from being relaxed to being tense and irritable. Then you started openly discussing your separate parts.

EP: Hmmm. I did, didn't I?

M: Yes. Now, tell me about how your parts keep information from each other.

EP: (Startled) Well, it happened just now. A minute ago,

one part of me actually denied the existence of the other parts; it didn't even want to acknowledge the possibility that they exist. It got angry. Another part is obviously willing to discuss this in great detail.

M: Very good.

EP: How many parts are there?

M: Four. Two you were born with, and two that developed after birth.

EP: Would you tell me about them?

M: Certainly. Some very clever Earth People have even given them names. The two you were born with are called the Natural Child and the Adult. The Natural Child is the source of all your feelings. It provides your emotional responses to life. It's intuitive, spontaneous, and creative, and it acts very much as a young child naturally would.

EP: Does it act like *I* did when I was a child?

M: Exactly. You've got the idea. The Adult part of you, on the other hand, has nothing to do with your age, nor with being grown up or mature—as its name might seem to imply. It's the computer in your head. It is the part of you that processes information, sorts data, and estimates probabilities. When you see clearly, you're seeing from your Adult. When you speak without coloring your words with emotion, or distorting them with some prejudice, you're speaking from your Adult.

EP: I get it! As I learn to see and hear like a Martian, what I'm really doing is developing, or strengthening, my ability to see and hear from my Adult!

M: That's right.

EP: What about my other two parts?

M: Your other two parts act as memory banks for the first two, although they often develop personalities all their own. One stores information, the other stores feelings.

EP: What are they called?

M: The one that stores information, and acts as a memory bank for the Adult, is, interestingly enough, called the Parent. This is because much of the information stored in your Parent came directly from your mother and father

—your own parents—when you were very young and unable to process data quickly with your own Adult. This information is often in the form of rules, regulations, and instructions on how to do things. This doesn't constitute *all* the information in your Parent, but it constitutes that part of the information that you yourself haven't thought through—which is what gives your Parent its own special character.

EP: I'll bet that a lot of this early information in my Parent is really incomplete or inaccurate—since I never got to think it through.

M: It certainly is. It's full of prejudices and other beliefs and distortions that are not grounded in fact.

EP: But didn't my *parents* think it through before they passed it on to me?

M: Not necessarily. Much of it came from their Parent, and had been passed down to them from the Parent in previous generations. *They* never got to think most of it through, either.

EP: And what about the fourth part of me, the part that stores feelings?

M: This part is called the Adapted Child. It's recorded all the feelings your Natural Child ever felt, and it remembers the situations in which you felt them. When these situations reoccur in your life, it often replays the early feelings automatically, at the same time that your Parent is replaying information about what to say and do. This often happens so rapidly that the average Earth Person is unable to distinguish between his Natural Child and his Adapted Child; or between his Adult and his Parent. He thinks he's responding spontaneously and actually processing information, when what he's really doing is responding automatically by playing a recording from his past. His responses are programmed and automatic.

EP: This must really cause problems!

M: You bet it does! Many people who are prejudiced —that is, operating from their Parent—think they're actually processing information and operating from their

Adult. Many others who feel depressed or frustrated—and may be operating from their Adapted Child—believe their discomfort is natural and can't be changed.

EP: But how can it be changed?

M: The memory banks act like tape recorders. The tapes can be turned off. New tapes can be inserted.

EP: Ah-hah! I remember you said earlier that Earth People could change their feelings—but that they didn't know they could. I thought you were crazy at the time, but now I think I see what you were talking about. You meant that they can turn off their tapes!

M: Yes.

EP: (Thinking seriously) Not many Earth People recognize they have these separate parts, do they?

M: No. Some recognize that when they get angry at someone the anger comes from a different part of them from the one that later apologizes. But that's about all.

EP: (Thunderstruck) That's really an awesome power to have—to be able to recognize the tapes!

M: It's even more awesome to be able to turn them off, to rearrange them and sort out your prejudices and beliefs; and to think through all the aspects of your life that you've previously ignored or blocked out.

EP: This is unbelievable! It can help me in *two* ways! I can see people around me more clearly, and I can see *myself* more clearly, too!

M: Right!

EP: The thing that intrigues me most is the way we got into this—by talking about how one part of me was hiding something from the others. That's absolutely fascinating! To think that a person can go around with one part of him not knowing what the other parts are doing!

M: It happens all the time. That's why most people don't become rich and happy. Their parts disagree, and pull against one another, rather than pulling *with* one another to obtain their mutual goals.

EP: (Pause) You mean if all my parts agreed, I could become rich and happy?

M: Yes.

EP: Wow!!! This is almost too overwhelming. I think I'll have to stop for a while and let it all sink in.

M: That's fine. You've learned a lot. We'll talk some more later.

Comments

1. This chapter introduces the rudiments of what, in Transactional Analysis, are called ego states. (My explanation differs somewhat from traditional T.A. teaching in that it gives full status to the Adapted Child as a separate ego state, or "part" of the personality.) I've found this basic model to be unequaled as a tool for achieving personal clarity. Of the many hundreds of people I've personally used it with, I've found that *all of them* could easily distinguish between their own ego states once they were acquainted with the process. This is a skill you can learn for yourself as you continue reading. It will become immeasurably valuable to you as you continue to examine your life plan, and as you alter it in order to become rich and happy.

2. One of the most important things you can learn from this book is the difference between your Adult and Parent, and between your Natural Child and Adapted Child. Many people succeed quite well in school, and even in business, through Adapted Child responses. At some point, however, they often find this method failing them, and they have no place to turn. Because of a lifetime of adaptation, they have difficulty breaking through the barriers of clarity, which requires the desire and energy of the Natural Child. (You have to *want* to do it!) Once you know your Natural Child, however, you will more easily be able to get on with the business of getting what you want. Very few successful people achieve their success through Adapted Child behavior, and those who do aren't very happy people.

3. Seeing these four ego states as separate parts that alternately surface and resurface, and alternately agree or

disagree or even hide things from each other, can provide you with a much clearer sense of how you operate than just about anything else you'll ever learn. These parts *are* separate, although you'll experience each of them as being "you." You might think they should automatically agree with each other, but there's nothing that says they have to, and in fact they frequently don't.

4. Most of your own life plan will be reflected in how and when your ego states surface, what they have to say, and how and when they deal with each other. The disagreements, differences, and blind spots will be particularly useful to note. People whose life plans lead directly to wealth and happiness have ego states that agree on almost all key issues. Their Parent contains all the things they "should" do, their Natural Child enjoys doing them, their Adapted Child doesn't resist or interfere, and their Adult processes all they need to know at a speed necessary to accomplish these things. To obtain riches, your goal will be to achieve this same efficient compatibility.

CHAPTER
SIX

EP Stops
Feeling Guilty

EP: Martian?

M: Yes.

EP: I've been thinking. A while back I said I needed some way to remember all these things I've been learning, and I've just figured out that you gave me one, by teaching me about the various parts people have. It's a sort of framework I can use to keep all these things in my mind.

M: I know.

EP: Did you do this on purpose?

M: Yes.

EP: How come?

M: You said you needed help.

EP: (Puzzled) But you didn't *say* you were going to give me any help.

M: I know.

EP: But *why* didn't you?

M: It was a gift.

EP: But you didn't even *tell* me!

M: So? You learned for yourself. Who says you must be told?

EP: You mean you give things to people without telling them?

M: Yes.

EP: Don't you want to be thanked?

M: What for?

EP: So you'll know the gift is appreciated.

M: If it's appreciated, I'll know. If it's not appreciated, I'll know that, too. What you say doesn't change what I know.

EP: But I'd feel guilty if I didn't thank you!

M: Remember when we talked about the separate parts of your personality?

EP: Yes.

M: Well, guilt is a feeling in your Adapted Child. You can stop feeling guilty if you want to. You can turn off the tape.

EP: But I don't need any fancy techniques to stop feeling guilty! All I need to do is thank you!

M: (Looking concerned, and thinking deeply, as if wondering whether or not to continue the discussion) When do you usually feel guilty?

EP: When I don't do something I know I should do.

M: Hmmm. It seems you need to learn more about your separate parts.

EP: Why do you say that?

M: So you can see how you arrange to feel certain feelings. You tie up lots of energy feeling things you don't have to. You could put this energy to more productive use.

EP: Like what?

M: Like arranging to get out of your confusion.

EP: But you *have* to feel guilty! You've got to have a conscience, and if you don't do what your conscience says you should, you should feel guilty!

M: (Hesitating) Do you want to learn more about these parts you have?

EP: Yes, but I also want to talk more about feeling guilty. I'm still not satisfied!

M: We can come back to that after you've learned more about your parts.

EP: Okay then, but don't forget!

M: I won't. Now . . . (Gathering his thoughts together) Each part has its own words, its own vocabulary, its own posture, and its own tone of voice. Each *looks* different from the others, and each is used for a different purpose.

EP: Really?

M: Yes. Your Parent is used to control, to protect, to punish, or to give permission. It says things like "you should," "you ought to," and "you have to." It has fixed positions and is unyielding. It operates on the basis of beliefs, and on rules and regulations passed down from other generations. It contains all the things you've been taught, and all you've learned for yourself and no longer think about. Your Parent doesn't think for itself. It typically sees things in black and white. It's judgmental and prejudiced. It's critical of views that conflict with its own. It deals in issues like morality and responsibility, and it usually talks in terms of good and bad and right and wrong. It's useful to you when you need to control a situation, or when you need to respond fast and automatically in situations that require no thought.

EP: What does my Parent look like?

M: Your Parent looks very much like a real mother or father dealing with a youngster. It frowns, or looks stern, and uses a powerful, controlling voice. It might even point an accusing finger at other people.

EP: And what about my Adult?

M: Your Adult is the computer in your head. It deals in probabilities. It asks questions and provides people with information. It assesses the data received. It talks about appropriateness, and examines options and alternatives. Your Adult makes decisions, but it doesn't judge. It's never tense. It has no urgencies. Your Adult isn't always visible on your face, but when it is, you're relaxed, alert, and aware. You look like you're listening or thinking—like you're processing data.

EP: And what about my Natural Child?

M: Your Natural Child smiles a lot. It says things like, "I like," and "I want," and "I feel." It wishes and dreams. It has fun. It enjoys life. It cries. It feels. It creates. It loves. It's curious. It's open and trusting. It responds spontaneously to the world around it. When you were young, *everything* you felt was a spontaneous Natural Child response to your immediate environment.

EP: (Seriously) And my Adapted Child?

M: Your Adapted Child sulks, and accommodates, and does all the things you *learned* to do as a little child. It's easily intimidated. It feels depressed, guilty, lonely, inept, and embarrassed. It may also feel angry, frustrated, or scared, as your Natural Child sometimes does, but your Adapted Child feels these feelings in situations where the feelings are unwarranted or unnecessary. Your Adapted Child's feelings are programmed and predictable—like when you get angry time and time again at the same thing.

EP: Are the feelings in my Natural Child and the feelings in my Adapted Child both *real* feelings?

M: Yes, in the sense that you genuinely *feel* them. Adapted Child feelings, however, are repeats from the past, which a person can choose not to feel anymore.

EP: I see.

M: Now, if you'd like, we can go back to our discussion about your feeling guilty.

EP: (Looking determined) Yes. I sure would. I think you were saying that people shouldn't feel guilty, and I don't agree.

M: Tell me once again when you usually feel guilty.

EP: When I don't do something I know I *should* do. Or, sometimes, when I do something I know I *shouldn't* do!

M: All right, now. Listen to your words. Do you hear your Parent—telling you what you should or should not do?

EP: What do you mean?

M: You just explained that you usually feel guilty when you don't do something you know you should do.

EP: I know that's what I said.

M: When you listened to these words, did you hear your Parent?

EP: Oh! (Pause) You mean *that's* my Parent?

M: Yes.

EP: Well, so what? Who cares what part of me says it? It's still what I should do.

M: Where did you learn about what you should and should not do?

EP: (Dumbfounded) Uh . . . I don't know. Everybody knows right from wrong.

M: Do you hear your Parent again?

EP: Again?

M: Did you hear it saying everybody knows right from wrong?

EP: I don't know what you're trying to tell me. Maybe everybody doesn't know right from wrong, but they certainly should!

M: Do you hear it still?

EP: What are you talking about?

M: I'm asking you about your perceptions. I want to know if you hear yourself. I want to know if you can tell me which part of you is speaking.

EP: Which part of me is speaking? Well, it's *me! I'm* speaking. *That's* which part is speaking.

M: I know it's *you* speaking. But do you remember which part of you is unyielding, says "you should" a lot, and talks about right and wrong?

EP: You said it was my Parent.

M: Yes. Now, in your conversation, did you hear your Parent speaking?

EP: (Flabbergasted) Oh, my God!! That was *it!!* I was just doing it. I was speaking from my Parent!

M: Right. It took a while for you to hear it.

EP: Hmmm. (Thoughtfully) But what do you do in a situation like that? You have to know what's right and wrong, and what you should and should not do.

M: Who says?

EP: But if you didn't, the world would be in chaos.

M: Here we go with *that* again. You're discounting your Adult. You're denying the fact that you have an Adult which could decide what would be best for you.

EP: Oh. You mean rather than just automatically thanking someone for a gift, I'd start thinking it through each time? I'd go crazy! It seems to me that would be very inefficient.

M: You'd only have to think the whole process through once, and then re-Parent yourself with your new conclusion.

EP: But I'd be right back where I started—in my Parent.

M: Yes, but now your Adult would have instant access to your Parent if you wanted to alter things in the future. You'd be able to constantly test your Parent for its effectiveness, and change it at will.

EP: I'm not sure I haven't been doing that all along. Most of my thoughts on thanking people for gifts are Adult, or based on Adult thinking.

M: Okay. Let's assume you *did* think this notion through with your Adult. Can you tell me what considerations you had in mind?

EP: Well . . . I usually thank people because it's the polite thing to do. It's just good manners.

M: So?

EP: What do you mean, "so"? That's the reason! That's what I had in mind when deciding to be polite. My Adult decided that it was good manners.

M: What's so important about politeness and good manners?

EP: Are you saying I shouldn't be polite?

M: I'm not *saying* anything. I'm asking a question. I don't substitute questions for statements like Earth People do. When I want to say something, I make a statement about it.

EP: Then what was your question?

M: The question was, "What's so important about politeness and good manners?"

EP: (Earnestly) It's courteous.

M: So? Why be courteous?

EP: (More earnestly) So people will be courteous in return. You can't expect courtesy unless you give it.

M: Is that the way it works? Whenever you're courteous to people, they're courteous in return?

EP: No. Not always. But most of the time.

M: What happens when people aren't courteous in return?

EP: I just don't deal with them anymore. I say to hell with them!

M: You get angry.

EP: (Sharply) Damn right!

M: Because you expected them to be courteous.

EP: Uh-huh. But I expect *myself* to be courteous, too!

M: And when you aren't courteous, you feel guilty?

EP: Right!

M: Do you hear all this?

EP: I *think* I do.

M: It's all from your Parent.

EP: My Parent?!! I thought I was giving you my Adult reasons for all this . . . .

M: It's all Parent. It's all the rules you've been taught about being polite, and courteous, and having good manners. You even thank people for gifts you don't *want* to receive, don't you?

EP: I sure do. Particularly my in-laws. Last year my mother-in-law gave me a huge house plant that takes gallons of water. I have to water it every day, and it's really *big!* It's a nuisance. I not only *thanked* her for it, but the only reason I kept it is to be polite. I really hate the thing!

M: And you become angry whenever you think of it.

EP: That's for sure!

M: Okay. Let's review what you said, so you can hear it. (Speaking carefully) You *expect* yourself to be polite. Sometimes you are polite—like with your mother-in-law—and then you feel angry. Sometimes you aren't polite—when you think you *should* be—and then you feel guilty. Sometimes *other* people aren't polite—when you think they should be—and then you feel angry again.

EP: (Tentatively) Yes. I think that's how it works . . .

M: Do you hear how you set these feelings up with your expectations? All you need to do is *expect* something—in this case politeness and good manners—and if it doesn't happen, you click in with certain programmed feelings.

EP: Yes. I hear that. And it really happens that way, too.

M: Well, all these feelings are in your Adapted Child.

They go hand in hand with your expectations, which are in your Parent. Your Parent and your Adapted Child operate together at such moments. Your Adult and your Natural Child are simply not involved. Your Parent tells you what you should do, and then your Adapted Child feels what you once learned to feel in similar situations. It's all programmed. It's all on tape.

EP: So? What's wrong with that? It's not so bad.

M: Nothing's wrong with it, unless you want to see clearly and arrange your life more to your liking.

EP: But how does it prevent me from rearranging my life?

M: When you're operating from your Parent or Adapted Child, you're not *seeing*. You haven't the faintest chance of seeing until you get into your Adult or Natural Child.

EP: Oh . . . (Thinking) Well, how can I *do* that?

M: You use your Adult.

EP: But I thought I was using my Adult. Apparently I wasn't, but since I don't seem to know the difference, I'm presented with something of a dilemma.

M: What do you want to do about the plant your mother-in-law gave you?

EP: I want to get rid of it.

M: *Will* you?

EP: I'd feel guilty.

M: But you feel *angry* now, whenever you think about it.

EP: I know.

M: Do you want to continue feeling angry?

EP: No. (Sounding concerned) But how would I explain it to my mother-in-law?

M: Explain what?

EP: Getting rid of the plant.

M: You could tell her what you actually did with the plant. You could say, "I got rid of the plant."

EP: But she'd ask why.

M: Then you could *say* why. You could say, "Because I wanted to," or "Because it was too much trouble to water every day."

EP: But then she'd think I didn't appreciate it.

M: See how you stop yourself from doing what you want? You bother about what other people think. Why not just say, "I appreciated your gift, but it caused me problems, so I got rid of it."

EP: Then she'd feel hurt.

M: So?

EP: She'd blame *me!*

M: So?

EP: I'd feel guilty.

M: Why?

EP: Because I'd hurt her.

M: Ah. That's another of your fantasies—you believe you can control what other people feel. Actually, your mother-in-law has her own Natural Child and her own Adapted Child. *She* controls what she feels, not you. You have no magical power over her.

EP: Well, she'd certainly *appear* hurt! I know her! That's exactly what she would do. She'd look, act, and sound as if she were hurt!

M: And which part of her would be doing it?

EP: Probably her Adapted Child.

M: Right. Now, is that what you'd feel guilty about—the fact that she replays some feeling tape from her past?

EP: (His face slowly lighting up) My God! I never thought of it that way! That's ridiculous. She's just trying to get her own way! She doesn't have to feel hurt if she doesn't want to!

M: And do you have to feel guilty?

EP: No!

M: Good. You've sorted most of that out.

EP: Wow! (Pregnant pause) That's really great. I'm not in my Parent anymore, and my Adapted Child doesn't have to feel guilty. How did you get me to do it?

M: I asked you what you *wanted* to do about your plant. As I said earlier, it's all in knowing what you want.

EP: (Thoughtfully) But before, when I was in my Parent, I didn't know what to do about it. I hadn't the faintest idea how to work it out!

M: We were talking abstractly, about the broad issue of

being polite. It's a Parent issue, and your Parent doesn't know anything about what you want. In order to change an earlier decision, you must have a specific issue you want to do something about. In this case it was the plant; or, more accurately, the feelings of anger and guilt you carried around with you regarding the plant.

EP: Did you know that right from the beginning?

M: Yes. I knew you were interested in something to do with gifts. Then you changed the subject to this *specific* gift your mother-in-law had given you. You just weren't clear enough at the time to say exactly what it was you were trying to figure out.

EP: Yes. I remember.

M: Next time, will you try to start out more clearly, rather than ask vague questions?

EP: Yes, I will.

M: Good.

EP: And you know what else I'll do?

M: No, I don't. Would you like to tell me?

EP: Yes, I would. I'll just give away that house plant my mother-in-law gave me. And if she asks me why, I'll tell her it was just too much of a nuisance.

M: And you won't feel guilty?

EP: (Smiling) *No way!*

M: Congratulations! You've learned a lot.

Comments

1. You now have an outline of how to listen for (and recognize) your Parent, and how to begin to deal with your Adapted Child feelings. The subject chosen to explore this process (expressing appreciation for unwanted gifts, and the related guilt feelings) isn't really a big issue for most people, yet it's the kind of issue that pops up randomly (just as it did for EP). I chose it specifically for that reason.

Handling issues as they randomly surface, regardless of their apparent significance, is the *only way* you can adequately explore the material in your Parent and Adapted

Child! Waiting for some big issue to cross your mind will only prevent you from starting. (There's too much to be explored for you to wait.) Smaller issues are almost always reflections of larger ones, and, as we'll see shortly with EP, the same *feeling* he uses to make sure he "thanks" people is the one he uses to prevent himself from getting rich.

2. Guilt is an Adapted Child feeling we use to control behavior. Mothers and fathers instill it in children (both knowingly and unknowingly) to manipulate them more easily. These children grow up and become adults whose Parent ego states continue to use this guilt (now programmed in their Adapted Child) to control their own activities and manipulate their own behavior, often against their will. Feeling guilty and feeling happy are mutually exclusive. (If you're feeling guilty, there's no way you can feel happy at the same time.) Furthermore, if you're engaged in some compulsive behavior to either relieve your guilt feelings or avoid them (like apologizing, or thanking people for things, or controlling your behavior in advance so you won't feel guilty afterward), you've got your energy tied up in ways that will ultimately defeat your efforts to see clearly. (You undoubtedly do this not only with guilt, but with many other Adapted Child feelings as well.) You don't *need* to do this! You can control your behavior using your Adult and Natural Child, and rearrange your life more effectively at the same time.

3. Like most people, EP has a tendency to string together three or four assumptions to justify his feelings and behavior. ("I'm polite because it's courteous." "I'm courteous because it's good manners." "Good manners mean good relationships—people will be polite *back* to you.") As you get a feel for how he does this, notice how certain assumptions go hand in hand, and how they're always used to justify certain other programmed feelings. Notice also that as these justifications are exposed, the associated feelings disappear, since there's no longer any "reason" to feel them. (Every time M says "So?" he's pointing to another of EP's assumptions.)

This is an extremely important phenomenon! Without

Parent support for our Adapted Child feelings (in the form of assumptions and justifications), we'd *simply be unable to sustain them!* Unless we can justify what we feel, we usually won't feel it. (We usually *stop* feeling something as soon as we lose our justification for it.) Unfortunately, many assumptions are such an integral part of our daily living (and of our life plan) that questioning them often seems like heresy.

4. The following statements, for example, deal with what to feel in a given situation, and contain their own built-in assumptions: "You should feel guilty." "It's natural to feel depressed." "You have every right to feel angry." "I feel disappointed. I expected more." Even in the heat of the moment, none of these statements makes any sense, *except as justifications for the related feelings!* Yet most people certainly *think* they make sense, and use them to sustain their feeling responses and maintain the forward momentum of their life plan. (There's no need to *change* what you feel if you can still justify feeling it to yourself.)

Compare these Parent justifications to what your Adult might say under the same circumstances: (a) "You *may* feel guilty, if you've been programmed that way, but you don't *have* to feel guilty. Some people are programmed with less guilt than others, anyway; and some get along very well with hardly any." (b) "It's natural to feel depressed only in depressing surroundings, like trying to survive as a homeless child in Bangladesh. Feeling depressed for most people in Western society isn't natural, it's adapted." (c) "You feel what you feel. If you're angry, then you're angry; but if it doesn't serve you, you can give it up." (d) "People feel disappointed whenever their expectations don't come to pass. If you don't like feeling disappointed, think in terms of probabilities, and you won't feel either surprised *or* disappointed."

5. One particularly troublesome assumption people often make is that they can control what other people feel. And conversely, that others can control what *they* feel. ("He made me angry." "She made me sad." "I hurt his feelings.")

This assumption so permeates our culture that it's almost impossible to find someone not influenced by it. Yet it's contrary to what actually happens. While you may appear to gain manipulative power over others by believing that you can make them angry, sad, happy, etc., such power usually creates more problems than it solves. (You become "responsible" for what they feel, and have to "be careful" not to "hurt" them. You also permit *them* to "hurt" *you!*) These activities drain away enormous amounts of time and energy which could be utilized to get rich, as well as create many of the dysfunctions that stand in the way of happiness.

CHAPTER
SEVEN

How to Decide
to Get Rich

EP: Martian, I've been doing some more thinking.

M: About what?

EP: Well, we've been talking a while now, and I remember your saying that in order to learn to see like a Martian I'd have to sort of go through a process.

M: Yes.

EP: And I could use the exact same process to become rich and happy, if I wanted to.

M: That's right.

EP: Well, I know I've only just started, and I may not have a good feel for the process yet, but I've been trying to figure out how someone could use it to get rich.

M: And?

EP: I just can't figure it out. None of this has anything to do with getting rich. If there's a connection, I sure as hell don't see it.

M: The connection is that everyone who gets rich has a plan, a plan he originally conceives in his own mind. We're in the process of clearing up your mind so you'll be able to conceive your own plan for riches, if you want to.

EP: You mean everyone who gets rich goes through all this?

M: Not necessarily. Some people decide to get rich when they're very young, and then just go out and do it.

EP: So, why can't *I* just decide to go out and do it?

M: You can if you want to.

EP: Well, I could *say* I wanted to, but I doubt that I could go out and do it.

M: That's because the decisions you've already made about your life would interfere with this decision. Before you can get rich you must first uncover the old decisions you once made that now stand in your way, and you must do something about them.

EP: I don't understand.

M: You have ways of operating your life which are locked in your Parent and your Adapted Child and which interfere with your progress. You have to turn the tapes off and put in some new ones before you can get rich.

EP: Oh. You mean people who just go out and get rich have a whole different set of tapes from me? Like, they're not worried about being polite; or they don't feel guilty about the same things I do; or maybe they don't feel guilty at all?

M: That's right.

EP: Yeah. (Pause) I'll bet they're really ruthless. They probably don't care anything at all about people.

M: Why do you say that?

EP: That's the way most rich people are. Money-grubbing. They take from people. Con men and people like that.

M: Sounds like you were taught that somewhere. I hear it coming from your Parent.

EP: You do?

M: Yes. Would you be comfortable with a lot of money?

EP: What do you mean?

M: Would you feel comfortable with money, as opposed to feeling embarrassed or guilty?

EP: Well, I wouldn't want to keep it all for myself. If I got rich, it would be so I could give the money away. I'd want to do good with it.

M: Were your parents rich?

EP: No. Of course not. But you already know that.

M: Did they think that rich people were con men, that you can't get rich honestly?

EP: I don't remem— Yes! My father used to talk about the robber barons, and how people who got rich always took from the poor.

M: Oh.

EP: And it's true! There's only a certain amount of money in the world, and in order to get more than your share you have to take from *somebody!*

M: Suppose they just *gave* it to you?

EP: Why would they do that, unless they were tricked? People don't give money away.

M: *You* would, if you were rich.

EP: What do you mean?

M: You just said that if you were rich you'd give your money away.

EP: Oh . . .

M: (Pause) Is it possible you got some of your ideas about money from your father?

EP: Yes, it is . . .

M: And that these ideas went into your Parent?

EP: It's possible.

M: And that you use such ideas as a justification for keeping yourself poor?

EP: What do you mean?

M: When we finished our last conversation, you said you were going to start out more clearly next time. Remember?

EP: Yes.

M: Would you do so, right now?

EP: How?

M: You started this conversation wondering about how this process might be used to get rich. Right?

EP: Yes.

M: Rather than just wondering about that somewhat abstract idea, would you be willing to make a clear statement about what you want?

EP: Sure. I would if I could.

M: Good. I'll wait.

EP: What do you mean?

M: You said that you'd make such a statement if you could. I know you can. So I'll wait.

EP: How long?

M: Until you make it.

(Several moments later)

EP: (Very quietly) I want to be rich.

M: I didn't hear you.

EP: (Slightly louder) I want to be rich!

M: I still can't hear you. What did you say?

EP: (Very loud) I want to be rich!!!

M: Oh.

EP: *Now,* did you hear me?

M: Yes. You said you want to be rich. You said it so softly at first I had a hunch you didn't want to hear yourself.

EP: But why wouldn't I want to hear myself?

M: Why did you speak so softly?

EP: Oh . . . (Thinking) You mean so maybe I could keep it from myself?

M: Does that seem to fit?

EP: Well, it *is* pretty stupid of me to want to get rich. *I* couldn't get rich!

M: Why not?

EP: I'm just not capable.

M: Oh?

EP: Yeah. I don't have what it takes.

M: Tell me about it.

EP: To get rich, you have to be motivated. You have to be a self-starter. You have to have creative ideas. You have to have a talent for such things.

M: That's very interesting.

EP: Why do you say that?

M: Do you hear your Parent scolding you—saying you're no good, you're not capable, and you don't have what it takes? And *also* saying you're not motivated, you're not a self-starter, you don't have creative ideas, and you don't have any talent?

EP: I didn't hear my Parent. Those are just things I said about myself.

M: But which *part* of you was saying them about which *other* part of you?

EP: Oh. (Thinking) You mean it was my Parent talking about one of the other parts of me?

M: Yes. Whenever you find yourself making judgments, or assumptions, it's your Parent. And when you're saying *bad* things about yourself, your Parent's scolding you, just like your mother or father once did.

EP: What part of me said I wanted to be rich?

M: You already know the answer to that question.

EP: Yes, I do. (Pause) It was my Natural Child.

M: That's right. Why did you say it so quietly?

EP: Hmmm. Now that you mention it, it seemed like I didn't want my Parent to hear. But *you* made me keep saying it louder and louder. Why did you do that?

M: So we could get your Parent to respond.

EP: Oh. And say all those nasty things about me?

M: Yes.

EP: But why?

M: So you could hear the voices in your head. In order to know where you are, you must first be able to hear the voices in your head.

EP: (Face lighting up) Yeah! I remember your saying that when we first started talking. I guess I didn't quite know what you were talking about.

M: But you're learning well. So far, we've learned you want to be rich, but your Parent gets after you whenever you suggest it. Apparently, your Parent doesn't like the idea of your getting rich.

EP: Why is that?

M: Remember earlier, when you said you may have gotten some of your ideas about money from your father?

EP: Yes.

M: Could it be your father didn't want you to make money?

EP: I guess it could, but I don't understand why.

M: *He* didn't have money, did he?

EP: No, he didn't.

M: He didn't know how to get it, did he?

EP: He knew only one way—taking it from the poor.

M: Would it have been a threat to him if *you* got rich?

EP: A threat? Not that I know of. He *wanted* me to succeed!

M: Could it have been that part of him wanted you to succeed, and part of him would have been threatened if you got rich?

EP: (Thoughtfully) I suppose so . . .

M: What part of him wanted you to succeed?

EP: His Natural Child.

M: What part was threatened?

EP: Probably his Adapted Child. (Pause) But why would that be?

M: You tell me. You knew your father better than I did.

EP: Well, he was the man in the family—the breadwinner. He spent his whole life struggling. Making money was hard work for him. It would have blown his mind to see it come easy to me.

M: Let's examine that a little. Who supported his role as the man in the family?

EP: My mother.

M: Oh?

EP: Yeah. I guess *she* didn't want me to get rich, either. She was always telling me not to upset my father. Not to disturb him.

M: Is the thought of getting rich scary to you?

EP: (Hesitating) Yes. It really is.

M: Would you feel guilty if you became rich?

EP: Very much so.

M: What's that about?

EP: Well, I don't know why I'd be scared, but I'd feel guilty because I'd be doing well at the one thing my Dad couldn't do at all. I'd be making him look bad.

M: So why feel guilty?

EP: Well, that's obvious. It's like hitting a man when he's down.

M: But what's the relationship between that and your feeling guilty?

EP: What do you mean? Don't you understand? I'd be doing something I *shouldn't* do! I'd feel guilty!

M: What shouldn't you be doing?

EP: Getting rich!!!

M: (Pause) Did you hear your Parent?

EP: Hmmm. (Somewhat startled) I certainly did. That's crazy. I just heard myself say I shouldn't get rich.

M: Yes. Your Parent sure doesn't like the idea, does it?

EP: It sure doesn't. That's really amazing.

M: Do you know what it's about?

EP: I guess it has to do with the fact that if you kick a man when he's down, you can really hurt him. I know it would really crush my father for me to get rich.

M: Do you hear that? It's your fantasy about how you can control people's feelings. You can't crush your father!

EP: Son of a gun! It's the same problem I had with my mother-in-law and that plant she gave me! I believe I can hurt people with my actions. I believe I control what they feel. But in a way, I *do* control what they feel. I *trigger* their feelings, even if I don't absolutely control them.

M: *They* trigger their feelings. Your action provides a stimulus, which they don't have to respond to. The choice of responding or not is theirs.

EP: But they may not *know* they have that choice.

M: That's true. Earth People usually aren't taught they have a choice.

EP: Even if I told them, they wouldn't understand!

M: It's like I said when we first met—most people choose not to hear many things that would be of value to them.

EP: There's not much I can do about that, is there?

M: No. There's *nothing* you can do about it. It's their problem, not yours.

EP: I guess I'm already clearer than I thought.

M: You're well on your way. (Pause) But let's get back to the business about your father. Which part of him did you say would feel hurt if you were to become wealthy?

EP: His Adapted Child.

M: And that's what you'd feel guilty about—the idea that your father might play an old tape about how bad he felt?

EP: (Sheepishly) It really sounds dumb when you put it that way.

M: But *is* that what you'd feel guilty about?

EP: Yes, it is. (A bit astonished at the admission)

M: Are you going to continue to feel guilty about it?

EP: (With determination) No. I'm not!

M: Good. Why do you think your Dad would play an old tape about feeling hurt?

EP: I don't know. He could have made money, if he'd wanted to.

M: How did he stop himself?

EP: Well, mainly he treated everybody as if they were honest, and as a consequence he got taken a lot.

M: Anything else?

EP: (Thinking) Really, when you get right down to it, he was just plain scared.

M: Oh?

EP: Yeah. I don't know why. He could have been rich if he hadn't been scared.

M: Do you think he knew that?

EP: Not to speak of . . . but maybe deep down inside he did.

M: And if he *had* known it, what would your getting rich have shown him?

EP: That it was easy. That *he* could do it, too.

M: Would he have liked that?

EP: It would have blown his cover. It would have shown him there was no need to be scared.

M: But would he have liked it?

EP: His Natural Child would have liked it. His Natural Child would have *loved* it. He would have been so relieved!

M: And his Adapted Child?

EP: His Adapted Child was the part of him that was always scared. My getting rich would have shown my father that he had no need for his Adapted Child. His Adapted Child would have hated me. (Pause) That's strange, isn't it?

M: No. It's very common. Each part of a person develops its own personality, and fights tooth and nail for its own survival.

EP: Even if that part is detrimental to the person?

M: *Especially* if that part is detrimental to the person—because then its survival is more likely to be at stake.

EP: Gee. That's really amazing.

M: Yes, I know. Now, consider this. Could *this* be why you've been afraid to get rich?

EP: Because my Dad's Adapted Child would have hated me?

M: Yes.

EP: Hmmm. That's really heavy. (Thinking deeply) But I'll bet you have something there. That hatred would have been really intense. It would have been enough to scare anybody.

M: So. Is this beginning to make sense to you?

EP: Somewhat, but not entirely.

M: Well, before I can explain further, there's one more thing you must know. You need to know that you once made a decision to avoid certain feelings like fear and guilt.

EP: How do you know that?

M: I hear it in your words. You say things like "I wouldn't do that because I'd feel guilty" and "I won't do this because it's too scary." You imply that the reason you don't do things is you want to avoid the feelings. You're not alone, though. It's very common.

EP: And it makes sense! Who would want to feel such feelings?

M: You may *think* it makes sense, but look at the problem it's caused you!

EP: What problem?

M: Well, you decided that if you ever became rich you'd undoubtedly feel guilty and scared. Guilty, because you believed you could control what other people felt, and therefore you'd "hurt" your father. Scared, because you believed part of him would then hate you. Since you'd already decided to *avoid* feeling scared and guilty, you had no alternative but to decide not to get rich.

EP: (His mouth hanging wide open) Well, that's amazing! (Pause) I heard every word you said, and it seems to be exactly what I've done. I see what you mean about *decisions* being so important. I really did decide all that!

M: You're catching on.

EP: I sure am! (Pause) But why was my *father* so afraid of making money?

M: Why have *you* been so afraid?

EP: What do you mean?

M: Think.

EP: (Pause) Well . . . I . . . oh, my God! You mean to say *he* was afraid because he thought his father would hate him—he had the same problem with my grandfather that I had with *him*?!!

M: Interesting, isn't it?

EP: (Completely dumbfounded) It's absolutely unbelievable! To think that something like this can actually be passed down from generation to generation!

M: You can be the first to break the chain.

EP: (Pregnant pause) You really think I can?

M: You can if you want to.

EP: (Eyes gleaming) How do I go about it?

M: By making some new decisions.

EP: Hmmm. I guess the decisions I really need to make involve feelings like guilt and fear. *Avoiding* them doesn't help me. But what do I do instead? Just *feel* them? That doesn't sound so smart!

M: You got into the habit of avoiding them because you thought you had no alternative to feeling them in certain situations. But you *do* have an alternative. Rather than working on your avoidance, you can work on your alternatives.

EP: What do you mean?

M: *You're* the one who sets up these feelings. You can examine how you do this, and decide not to do it anymore. Then you'll have nothing to avoid.

EP: But *how* can I do that?

M: You don't need to ask me how. You already know.

EP: What do you mean?

M: You stopped feeling guilty about keeping the plant your mother-in-law gave you. How did you do *that*?

EP: I decided I didn't *have* to keep the plant. I'm not in charge of what my mother-in-law feels.

M: Okay. (Pause) What part of you says you *have* to do things?

EP: My Parent.

M: So what part of you did you change?

EP: (Thinking deeply) My Parent!! I must have switched a tape! I changed my Parent from "I *have* to keep the plant" to "I *don't* have to keep the plant."

M: How?

EP: Well, I used what you told me about people's separate parts. I decided since I don't control what my mother-in-law feels, there's no need for me to keep the plant. I'll just get rid of it, and if she feels hurt, that's her problem. She doesn't *have* to feel hurt.

M: What part of you wanted to get rid of the plant?

EP: My Natural Child.

M: And how did your Natural Child deal with your Parent?

EP: It enlisted the aid of my Adult.

M: Very good.

EP: And my Adult thought it over and told my Parent it was crazy. All of a sudden I didn't have to keep the plant anymore. I felt like a restraint had been lifted.

M: Like you had permission to do something you'd always wanted to do?

EP: Yes.

M: And what about the guilt in your Adapted Child?

EP: It was no longer relevant.

M: Okay. *That's* the process! You've already gone through it once. You didn't even have to ask me how.

EP: (Pause) You're right. I didn't, did I?

M: Right. And that's why I said you eventually won't need me.

EP: You mean I can use this process for *all* my problems, and I can do it without your help?

M: Yes.

EP: (Gleefully) Wow! Let's see now. The way it works is—my Natural Child decides what I want, and gets my Adult to help. Then they both go to work on my Parent, which then turns off my Adapted Child. Right?

M: You've got it. The key thing is to decide what you want, and to *see* how your Parent and Adapted Child prevent you from getting it.

EP: Oh. Yeah. I use my Natural Child to decide what I want, and I use my Adult to see *what* my Parent and Adapted Child are doing to prevent my getting it.

M: Right. Only then can you get your Parent to give you permission to go ahead.

EP: Okay. I know I've got it now. Let's call it a day. I've got about all I can handle at one sitting. All right?

M: Fine with me.

Comments

1. For the first time in this book we're dealing directly with the issue of money. People *do* stop themselves from getting rich for reasons related directly to money, but they're rarely the most important reasons. Dealing with them prematurely could be misleading. A person usually needs to learn about *seeing* and *hearing* before he can know what to do about issues related to money.

2. The difficulties EP faces in this chapter are common

to many people. The average person doesn't *know* how to make large sums of money, and he typically fantasizes in unrealistic ways about how others do it. He often uses his *negative* fantasies to justify his own inaction. (Rich people rob from the poor, and *he* wouldn't want to rob from the poor. Rich people are all con men, and *he* wouldn't want to cheat people.)

If you check yourself out, you'll find you harbor many such ideas. You may realize that they're not all grounded in fact—that is, your Adult may realize it—but your Child may cling to them nevertheless. If you're excruciatingly honest with yourself (which you need to be in these matters), you might see yourself clinging to one or more of the following notions:

(a) People who get rich are lucky.
(b) People who get rich are talented.
(c) People who get rich are unusually talented and lucky.
(d) People who get rich have the right connections.
(e) People who get rich sacrifice too much.
(f) People who get rich don't enjoy their money.
(g) People who get rich are cold and unfeeling.
(h) People who get rich are self-centered and miserly.

3. Even more important are the Parent notions people have about *themselves* ("I'm just not capable." "I don't have what it takes." "I can't make it."), and the Adapted Child feelings these notions evoke (ineptness, guilt, and depression).

When you have a moment, sit down and list all the adjectives you can think of to describe yourself, and all the feelings you feel in any given day (as nearly as you can pinpoint them). Many of them may sound foolish (to your Parent) or feel embarrassing (to your Adapted Child), but they exist in *all* of us, and you need to *know* what they are if you're ever going to get a handle on how you live your life. (If you start resisting, make a note of how you go about it, so you can get a feel for how you prevent yourself from knowing.) Take special note of those adjectives and feelings that *limit* you, or stand in your way, which you want to eliminate from your life.

4. By far our greatest long-term difficulties come from decisions we made as youngsters in order to deal with the Parent and Adapted Child of our own mother and father. (Deciding not to do things that might threaten our parents is the most common.) Since almost all mothers and fathers operate from a lot of distorted information (in their Parent) and irrational feelings (in their Adapted Child), it's *inevitable* that at one time or another you responded to their mixed messages and irrational fears by making dysfunctional decisions of your own. (The decisions weren't dysfunctional *then*, but they are *now* that you've grown up and moved away.)

To get a more accurate feel for how your parents influenced you about money, close your eyes and picture a scene where you return home and announce to your mother and father that you've just figured out how to get rich and you've made a million dollars (or whatever else is appropriate for you). Picture your parents not as you know them now, but as they were when you were seven or eight years old. Watch their faces and listen to their responses. Are they interested, happy, indifferent, angry, scared? Is one happy but the other scared? Do they start telling you what to do with the money? Do they beg you to give them some? Do they punish you for being greedy or materialistic? Do they belittle your efforts? Are they overly concerned with how it might affect them, or do they smile and encourage you to make even more?

Any scene that involves nonacceptance of any sort is one which a little person would certainly try to avoid. Any scene that involves encouragement is one he'd try to repeat. If *you* received anything other than Natural Child acceptance or encouragement, you know what influenced you (and *still* influences you) to decide against making money.

5. Before leaving this chapter, it might be worthwhile to take a look at M's method of questioning. All his questions have a purpose—to help EP know what he feels, to help him

decide what he wants, to get him to *say* what he wants, to help him see how his Parent and his Adapted Child stop him from getting what he wants, and to help him explore and change the early decisions that motivate his current actions. The majority of these questions, as you can see from their wording (what do you feel, what do you want), are directed to EP's Natural Child.

CHAPTER EIGHT

Finding Your Own Pace

EP: Boy, this gets more and more fascinating, the more I learn!

M: What are you speaking of?

EP: Well, we started our last conversation talking about how this process of getting clear could be used to get rich. We never did finish that conversation, but in the meantime I think I've learned the key to happiness!

M: Really? Tell me about it.

EP: Well, look at it this way. Some people say happiness is a state of mind, but it's *more* than that. I think it's really a feeling, or more accurately, the absence of any *bad* feelings!

M: So?

EP: So, you've just shown me how I can get rid of all my bad feelings! I can turn off the tapes. Once I've done that, I'll have only good feelings left! I'll automatically be happy!

M: That's very perceptive. You may actually have to *turn on* some good feelings after you've eliminated the bad ones, but you've got the general idea.

EP: I think it's fascinating! The only problem is that I should be picking this up faster than I am. I'm taking too long.

M: Oh?

EP: Yes. We've been talking quite a while now, and I'm

really not much further along than when I started. Can't we possibly speed things up?

M: *You* were the one who stopped our last conversation. You felt you'd had enough.

EP: I know. I shouldn't have done that.

M: Why not?

EP: I was just slowing myself down. At that rate I'd take forever.

M: What's the rush?

EP: I don't *have* forever!

M: Have you always hurried so much?

EP: You know I have. You've been watching me.

M: I wanted to know if *you* knew. What's the purpose of your hurrying?

EP: Look. It may be different for *you,* but Earth People don't live forever. If you want to live life to the fullest and get the most out of it, you've got to keep moving.

M: Moving, I can understand. What I was wondering about was hurrying.

EP: What do you mean?

M: Well, you've been hurrying for years, hustling around—always on the go—as if you're really trying to get someplace fast. It seems to me that all you've done is hurry yourself into the mess you're in now. For all your hurrying, you haven't gotten very far.

EP: You really know how to hurt someone, don't you?

M: That's not my intent. I'm telling you what I see. Other people get much further without hurrying.

EP: The reason I hurry so much is that I've got a lot of things to do.

M: Things you *have* to do or things you *want* to do?

EP: Things I *have* to do! Life is not a bed of roses! Somebody's got to do these things!

M: Who says?

EP: *I* say!

M: And which part of a person says he *has* to do things?

EP: Hmmm. That would be his Parent.

M: And which part of *you* was just speaking?

EP: Oh . . . (Vaguely) My Parent, I guess.

M: You guess?

EP: (Somewhat disgusted) Okay. It was my Parent.

M: What was your Parent saying?

EP: Hurry up.

M: And why was it saying that?

EP: I don't know. It's *always* said that.

M: What were you *feeling* when your Parent was telling you to hurry?

EP: Anxious. Uneasy. Impatient.

M: And what part of you was feeling anxious, uneasy, and impatient?

EP: My Natural Child.

M: Oh? I'm not so sure. What makes you say that?

EP: Well, I'm not feeling guilty, or scared, or embarrassed, or some other Adapted Child feeling. I just want to get on with this, and that's *natural,* isn't it?

M: Which part of you was doing all the talking about hurrying?

EP: My Parent, like I said before.

M: And which *child* part of you pairs off with your Parent?

EP: Well, it's usually my Adapted Child.

M: It's *always* your Adapted Child.

EP: Oh. So you mean it was my Adapted Child that was feeling anxious and impatient?

M: Yes. What was it all about?

EP: Hmmm. (Pause) Well, I can't say I really know. At least, my Adult can't figure it out. My Parent has lots to say about it. My Parent says that slow people are lazy. They waste time. They never get things accomplished. It also says I shouldn't be that way. Whenever I hear it say that, I start feeling anxious. I try to speed things up.

M: What would happen if you stopped hurrying?

EP: (Blurts out) I'd live longer.

M: Oh?

EP: Yeah. This is a pretty stiff pace I keep up.

M: So why not slow down?

EP: Well, I don't expect to live so long, anyway. Everybody dies young in my family.

M: You don't want to live a long life?

EP: Not particularly. I've seen lots of old people. They get senile and can't take care of themselves. I wouldn't want that to happen to me.

M: Did your mother and father hurry a lot?

EP: Why do you ask?

M: You must have learned to hurry somewhere.

EP: Well, my mother did.

M: When did she die?

EP: Why do you want to know?

M: You said that *you'd* live longer if you stopped hurrying. Since *she* never stopped hurrying, I was wondering when she died.

EP: She died when she was fifty-five.

M: Suppose you'd stopped hurrying before she died. Would she have liked that?

EP: She wouldn't have had anything to do with me. She didn't wait for people to catch up with her. She kept moving.

M: And you stayed right with her?

EP: You bet I did!

M: Even when you were a youngster?

EP: Right.

M: And if you *hadn't* stayed with her?

EP: She'd have gone on without me.

M: Would you have cared?

EP: Cared? What are you talking about? Of course I would have cared. I didn't want her to *leave* me!

M: So, you started hurrying in order to keep up with your mother—to avoid being left behind.

EP: Right.

M: And you're still hurrying.

EP: Hmmm . . .

M: Did you hear yourself just now?

EP: Yes, I did. It sounded strange. Like the only reason I'm hurrying is to keep up with my mother, who's been dead now for a number of years.

M: That's right.

EP: That's weird! (Pause) If this keeps up, I'll be needing a psychiatrist pretty soon.

M: Okay. What I hear is that you geared the pace of your life to your mother's pace. It was *her* pace, not yours. It's almost as if her voice is still in your head, as part of your Parent, telling you to hurry up—and you're still complying. It made sense when you were young. It doesn't now.

EP: Is there something *really* wrong with it?

M: Your present pace is not a natural pace for you. It wasn't natural for your mother, either, but that's not important now. Everybody has a pace in life that is comfortable for him. It is *his* pace, and it can't be altered comfortably to suit someone else.

EP: Well, I'm comfortable with my present pace.

M: You said before that you felt anxious, uneasy, and impatient. Those are not comfortable feelings.

EP: Oh.

M: Do people seem comfortable to *you* when they're anxious, uneasy, and impatient?

EP: Not particularly. I wonder why *I* seem comfortable?

M: It's because your body has adapted. It's like smoking, when you inhale cigarette smoke with all kinds of impurities in it and say you enjoy it. After a while your body adapts to the discomfort and you believe it's comfortable.

EP: So, you're saying that my body has adapted to all this anxiousness, and now I *think* it's comfortable, even though it really isn't?

M: Exactly.

EP: Well, how in the world am I to know what's comfortable, and what's not, if my body can't tell the difference anymore?

M: This is what I was talking about earlier when I said you needed to learn more about what you feel. You can use your other perceptions. If you can't tell by feeling, try looking. See if you *look* comfortable.

EP: Oh. Okay. I get you. I can look in the mirror, or get a feel for my appearance—what I look like.

M: Right. Now, at what age do you think you might die?

EP: Oh, around fifty-five or sixty. What's that got to do with it?

M: You don't *have* to die then, you know.

EP: What do you mean by that? I'm not *planning* to die then. That's just when I think I *might* die.

M: You *are* planning to die then.

EP: That's ridiculous. What makes you say that?

M: Your pace.

EP: What do you mean?

M: You push yourself. Many people who push themselves die early. They hurry through life.

EP: You must have more to go on than just that.

M: You also told me earlier you'd live longer if you stopped hurrying. It's as if you *expect* to die early. The rationale you gave me was that people die young in your family. That's just a surface explanation. The real reason is that at some level you know you can't maintain your pace forever.

EP: Hmmm. Are you saying people actually decide when they'll die?

M: Yes. And barring accidents and other unforeseen catastrophes, they usually live just long enough to make their plan come true.

EP: Well, I know I don't want to live *too* long. I don't want to become old and senile.

M: People don't hurry through life just to avoid senility. They do it to keep up with their mother, or father, or somebody else in their early life. The decision to die early only helps them justify the pace.

EP: That's really crazy. Now I *know* I need a psychiatrist.

M: You don't need a psychiatrist. You need a redecision. You knew the decision to hurry wasn't healthy for you when you made it as a youngster. But since you had little choice about making it, you decided to justify it to yourself by not caring if you lived a long life. You went around collecting limited data on how it wouldn't be much fun to live long, anyway.

EP: What do you mean, limited data?

M: Many old people never become senile, and those who do may not become so until their eighties or nineties—or even later. You didn't look at *all* the old people around you. You looked only at a small group of them—those who would justify the decision you made.

EP: How can you tell the difference between the real reason a person does something and the false reason he uses to justify what he's already decided?

M: The real reasons have to do with survival. A person doesn't decide *against* himself—against living a long time, feeling good, or being happy—unless it's to survive.

EP: Ah-hah! And most of these survival situations occur when he's young, right?

M: Yes. And they almost always involve the big people around him—his mother, father, grandparents, older brothers and sisters, and any others with power and influence over him.

EP: Hmmm. (Pause) Well, since I need to make a redecision about the pace I use to run my life, how do I do it?

M: Look at the implications. If you continue hurrying, you'll die early. You'll keep feeling anxious, uneasy, restless, and impatient, instead of feeling comfortable, relaxed, and at ease. You'll have found the key to happiness—the knowledge about turning off your tapes—and never used it, all because you once made a decision to keep pace with your mother, and decided never to change it. You can, if you want, keep pace with her right to your grave.

EP: You make it sound pretty grim.

M: It is. You'll also never get out of the mess you're in. You need time to think. You need personal space. And you can't get the time and space you need if you're always hurrying around. You're the only one who can give yourself the time and space you need. No one else can. You thought your mother took it away from you, but you can take it back for yourself. The choice is yours.

EP: You make my mother sound really bad.

M: Mothers frequently don't know what they're doing. Neither do fathers. They mix the good with the bad. It isn't on purpose. It just happens that way.

EP: Well, if I decide to go ahead and do this, how do I go about it?

M: Turn off the Parent voice in your head—the voice that says hurry up. Accept the fact that you don't *need* to hurry anymore.

EP: It's that simple?

M: Yes. Once you decide.

EP: (Pause) Well, okay. Let's just take our time going through the rest of this process. *I* don't need to hurry if *you* don't. I also don't need to follow my mother right to the grave.

M: Okay. It's a deal.

Comments

1. Suppose you found out you could decide how and when you'd die! Suppose you found out you could actually *plan* how long you'd live (up to a maximum of about 120 years)! Would you be surprised? Would you be excited? Would you be interested in living that long?

Well, unless we're killed by an accident or natural disaster, most of us *do* decide how long we'll live. We do it by making many smaller decisions about our pace, about the stress we put on ourselves, about how we eat, and drink, and exercise, and smoke. (Take a moment and ask yourself—if you *had* to take a guess—at what age do you think you might die?) Most people have an age fairly close to the tip of their tongue, often with several reasons to substantiate it. (Family history, actuarial tables, and "heredity" are the most common.) These reasons, however, serve merely to justify their existing pace and life style. If you look closely, you'll see that the age you've selected for yourself pretty much fits the way you're handling yourself, the treatment you're giving your body, and the approximate time it takes human organs to break down under such treatment.

Most of the independent decisions you've made toward determining when you'll die can be redecided! (Those related to environmental stress, exercise, and general health habits are perhaps the most important.*) While this may not seem to be directly related to becoming rich and happy, another ten or twenty healthy years tacked onto your life can give you much more room to enjoy your ultimate wealth and happiness. It can also give you a bit more time to get there.

2. This chapter illustrates four basic elements present in many life decisions. They're present in *all* decisions involving Adapted Child feelings you might want to change. They are: (a) the decision itself ("I've got to hurry up to keep up with Mom."); (b) the Parent "driver"—that is, the Parent voice in your head which does the pushing, or driving, to implement the decision ("Hurry up. Hurry up."); (c) the Adapted Child feelings (anxiousness, uneasiness, and impatience); and (d) the Parent justifications used to support the decisions and feelings ("I don't have forever." "I want to live life to the fullest." "I've got lots of things to do.").

If you want to change how you feel, here's how to do it: first, pinpoint the feelings you want to get rid of; second, look for the driver and justifications; and third, decide how and when you'll give them up! The justifications are easiest to spot. (You can usually hear them in ordinary conversation.) The feelings may be harder to isolate (because they're sometimes submerged), but since *they're* what you're trying to get rid of in the first place, you'll usually be able to recognize them with just a little effort. The Parent driver may never be openly stated, as it was in this chapter, but it can often be inferred from the apparent purposefulness of your behavior. (Are you hurrying? Are you dragging your heels? Are you trying to please people? Are you going

---

*Some of the best information on this subject can be found in books available in most health food stores.

around in circles? Are you resisting?) The original decision itself may never be known, *but it doesn't have to be known in order to change your feelings and behavior!* (It's just *helpful* to know it, at times.)

3. The Parent driver is the one element not discussed in previous chapters. (The driver is the voice in a person's head that drives him forward.) It's very much like a justification, but it's *stronger* than most justifications, in the sense that even after the justifications are stripped away, the driver can still keep a person locked into its behavior. *The driver is the mechanism we use to activate our life decisions!*

We have many such drivers. Some of the more common ones are shown below, along with a few questions to ask yourself to see if they apply to you.

HURRY UP	Do I always seem to be rushing around, trying to catch up, afraid to miss something?
BE PERFECT	Do I feel bad when I "fail" at things or when I don't measure up? Do I *have* to do things precisely right? Am I so afraid to make mistakes that I only choose to do things I know I can succeed at?
PLEASE ME	Do I constantly seek other people's approval or acceptance? Do I feel uncertain or unsure by myself? Do I *always* try to please others before myself?
TRY HARD	Do I place a lot of value on how much effort I put into things regardless of the results?
BE STRONG	Do I always need to appear to have things under control? Do I need to "tough" things out?

We adopt these drivers because we know of no other way to operate! In order to give them up, it's important to learn that other ways of operating have equal validity. A person with a "be perfect" driver needs to know that it's okay to make mistakes. (In fact, it's essential, for there's no other way to learn.) A person with a "hurry up" driver needs to know that it's okay to take his time, and that he'll get there more comfortably if he slows down and enjoys himself. A person with a "please me" driver needs to know that his worth doesn't depend on what others think of him, and that he'll do better relying on himself. A person with a "be strong" driver needs to know that it's okay to feel and to be open. A person with a "try hard" driver needs to know that it's okay to finish things, or to succeed at them.

To be most effective, this information is best presented in the form of "permissions" that the person's Parent presently doesn't give him, but *needs* to give him so that he can unlock his dysfunctional behavior patterns. (Permission to make mistakes, to slow down, to depend on himself, to be open, and to succeed.) When you're working on your *own* Parent drivers, these will be the permissions you'll need to give *yourself*. No one else can do this for you.*

---

*For more detailed information on this subject, see the article by Taibi Kahler and Hedges Capers on p. 26 of the *Transactional Analysis Journal*, Vol. IV, No. 1, January, 1974. (For back copies of the *T. A. Journal*, write Transactional Pubs, 1772 Vallejo Street, San Francisco, California 94123. Single copies are $2.50.)

CHAPTER NINE

Changing What You Feel

EP: Martian?

M: Yes?

EP: I'm bored.

M: With what?

EP: I don't know. I've just spent the whole day feeling bored.

M: So?

EP: I just thought I'd mention it.

M: What did you have in mind in mentioning it?

EP: Nothing in particular. I just thought I'd mention it.

M: You're not being straight. The part of you that brought it up had a reason for doing so.

EP: What do you mean?

M: You have something in mind.

EP: No I don't. It was just something to say, something to start the conversation with.

M: Yes, but of all the things you might have said to start the conversation, you chose to say that you were bored. What's that about?

EP: Nothing! It's not about anything! I'm sorry I said it!

M: Oh?

EP: Yes! I wouldn't have said it if I thought I was going to get hassled.

M: Who's hassling you?

EP: You are! You're asking me to justify bringing it up. You're saying I have to have a reason!

M: You didn't hear me. I didn't say you had to have a reason. I said you *had* one, and I wondered what it was.

EP: Well, it's the same thing. They both mean I have to justify bringing the subject up—that I shouldn't have brought it up without a reason.

M: No. They don't mean the same thing. They're different statements. I didn't ask you to justify anything.

EP: You didn't? (Looking confused) Well, *I* think you did! It sounded that way to me!

M: But I didn't. Look, when you were young, did you always need to have a reason for doing things?

EP: How am I supposed to know? I don't remember everything that happened when I was young!

M: (Softly) Were you punished if you didn't have a reason?

EP: Well . . . (Hesitantly) I guess I was. That's why I'm sorry I brought the subject up. You're doing the same thing my parents always did—saying that I have to have a reason.

M: I'm *not* saying that. You're still not hearing me. (Pause) What part of a person says he *has to* have things, or he *has to* do things?

EP: His Parent.

M: Okay. You seem to be suggesting that *I'm* your Parent, saying you have to do something and making demands of you.

EP: Hmmm.

M: But I'm not your Parent. I'm not making demands of you. I'm not saying you have to do anything. It's your own Parent saying it to you, just like your mother and father used to do. Your own Parent is now very much like they used to be. You hassle *yourself*.

EP: You mean you didn't say I had to have a reason?

M: That's right. You only thought I did, because it's so indelibly etched in your own Parent. What I said was you *had* a reason, and I wondered what it was.

EP: But isn't that the same thing?

M: No. Your Parent made a demand of you. It said you *had* to have a reason, or you *had* to justify yourself. Your Adapted Child got scared because it didn't see any way of living up to the demand. *I* didn't make a demand of you. I made a statement of fact.

EP: What? That I had a reason for bringing the subject up?

M: Yes.

EP: Well if I do, I certainly can't think of it!

M: That doesn't mean you don't have a reason. It only means you'll feel scared if your *Parent* says you need one.

EP: I really *didn't* have a reason! I brought the subject up because I felt like it. I just wanted to.

M: But *that's* a reason, right there.

EP: What? That I *wanted* to bring it up?

M: Yes.

EP: Well, it's not a reason to most people! The people *I* know usually want a better reason than that!

M: Yes, I know. Yet it's really the best reason of all. It says your Natural Child is the source of your motivation.

EP: It never satisfied my mother and father.

M: I know. That's how they got you to do what *they* wanted. They didn't accept what *you* wanted. They nearly buried your Natural Child in the process.

EP: But I know lots of other people who don't accept it, either.

M: That's their problem, not yours. What's important is that *you* learn to accept it. You need to give yourself permission to do what you want.

EP: Why do you say that?

M: Because you don't have your own permission yet. Until you do, you'll use time and energy arguing with your Parent. Your Parent will place demands on you, and you'll get involved in complying, or rebelling, or arguing, or feeling angry or scared. Time spent dealing with your Parent will be unavailable for more productive uses.

EP: Well, how do I do it? How do I give myself permission?

M: Get your Parent off your back. Let yourself do what you want.

EP: You mean *anything* I want, whenever I want to do it?

M: Whatever it takes.

EP: Should I just ignore other people, and do what I want in spite of what they may think?

M: Do you hear yourself? You're asking *me* for permission. You're asking *me* what you should do. You need to have your *own* permission, not mine. I'll be here for your entire journey, regardless of what you do.

EP: But if I just go ahead and do what I want, I'll have some really bad arguments with my family, and with people at work!

M: So?

EP: They won't like it. I'll upset their plans. They'll want me to do what *they* want.

M: Will that be a problem for you?

EP: It sure will. I get into enough arguments as it is. I could get fired, or my wife might even divorce me.

M: So?

EP: What do you mean, "So?" That would be terrible!

M: Why?

EP: Are you kidding? I could lose everything!

M: If these people stop you from doing what you want, why do you want them around?

EP: Because I don't *want* to get fired or divorced! That would be disastrous!

M: Do you hear yourself?

EP: Huh?

M: Scaring yourself?

EP: You mean saying it's disastrous—that I could lose everything?

M: Yes.

EP: Well, I *could!*

M: You *could,* but not *necessarily.* It's not inevitable.

EP: But it's highly likely.

M: There are other possibilities.

EP: I can't think of any.

M: Do you want to continue scaring yourself?

EP: No.

M: Will you stop?

EP: I don't know if I can.

M: Sure you can! Let's examine how you get into it.

EP: Into what? Scaring myself?

M: Yes.

EP: (Pause) Well, I think about how terrible it would be to get fired or divorced—how awful it would be to lose everything.

M: What else do you think about?

EP: I think about how I don't have any other way to deal with my boss, or with my wife. Like, if I decide to do what I want, there's no alternative but disaster.

M: What part of you has dealt with them in the past?

EP: Well, it's hard to say. I guess it's mainly my Adapted Child, when you get right down to it. I'm usually compliant or angry—either rebelling or doing what I'm told.

M: Okay. So there *are* some possibilities for using your other parts in the future. Disaster may come if you continue to use your Adapted Child, but it may not come if you use your Adult.

EP: Hmmm. (Pause) It's hard for me to figure out what my Adult would say.

M: I know. It takes practice. But let's get back to how you scare yourself.

EP: Okay.

M: People who succeed in life think about the future—as you do—but they think about it in a different way. They don't think about the disaster that might occur if they were to use their Adapted Child. They think about the success that will be inevitable if they use their Natural Child and their Adult.

EP: They do?

M: Yes. And they *feel* something different, too. There's always a certain amount of nervous energy involved in anticipating the future. This energy can be turned into fear, by thinking of how your Adapted Child will handle things, or it can be turned into excitement and eagerness, by thinking of getting all you want out of life by using your Natural Child and Adult. People who succeed generate excitement. People who fail generate fear.

EP: That's interesting. You mean people use energy in both cases?

M: Yes. They use as much energy to stop themselves as they do to move forward and succeed. You've stopped yourself for quite a while, and it will take considerable energy and effort on your part to get out of your mess; but once you've started, you'll pick up momentum and the rest will come easy.

EP: That's good to know. Right now, just getting started seems almost impossible.

M: I know. That's an indication of how much energy you'll need to apply.

EP: And this way I've been stopping myself, or scaring myself—you think that it's energy applied in the wrong direction?

M: Yes. And you *learned* to do it that way, just as other Earth People learned how to keep themselves eager and excited.

EP: What's the key to generating this excitement?

M: Getting your Parent off your back. This excitement comes from your Natural Child, and right now your Natural Child is so stifled by your Parent that the energy doesn't even get a chance to surface. You need to back up and rid yourself of all your "shoulds," all your "ought-tos," and all your "have-tos." The energy you need comes from anticipating getting what you want, knowing your Parent won't intervene, and being confident that by merely continuing to do what you're doing, you'll *get* what you want.

EP: But how can I be sure I'll get what I want just by doing whatever I'm doing?

M: If what you're doing is using your Adult and Natural Child, and you continue to do so, it's inevitable.

EP: So it really boils down to knowing which part you're using, and making sure you stay with your Adult and your Natural Child.

M: Absolutely.

EP: Well, what about this boredom I've been feeling the past few days?

M: What about it?

EP: I was wondering if it was my Natural Child or my Adapted Child.

M: Which do you think it is?

EP: I'm not sure. I started feeling bored right after I decided to stop hurrying. I've collected a whole bunch of things to do and I don't seem to care if I do them.

M: So what's the problem?

EP: I'm not accomplishing anything.

M: So?

EP: I *want* to accomplish something! I don't want to just sit around doing nothing!

M: You're accomplishing something now.

EP: That's not what I mean. I don't *like* feeling bored! It's not helping me any!

M: Ah. Are you aware that this is the reason you brought the subject up in the first place—way back when you started this conversation and said you didn't have a reason?

EP: Hmmm . . . Yeah . . . I guess it is.

M: I was hoping to hear you say this when we first started the conversation. We couldn't work on your boredom until I knew you actually wanted to do something about it.

EP: Oh! That's interesting. I guess I wasn't very clear when we started talking. Somehow, I'm a lot clearer now.

M: Good. Now, what do you want to do?

EP: I want to stop feeling bored.

M: Okay. Let's examine how you get into it. Have you felt bored very often?

EP: Not really. I'm usually rushing around too much to feel bored.

M: Think back.

EP: (Pause) Well, when I was young I used to go on vacations with my folks. We went to the lake, and everyone would sort of hang around and act lazy.

M: Was it boring?

EP: Not really. I think I mainly felt lethargic. (Reflecting) Come to think of it, that's more like what I've been feeling lately. I've been feeling more lethargic than bored.

M: What was the purpose of feeling lethargic on your vacation?

EP: It sort of filled time. It was resting, and relaxing.

M: You liked it?

EP: Yes. After all the hurrying and hard work, it was a relief!

M: It sounds like it was something like a reward.

EP: Yes! That's what it was! You didn't have to go anywhere or do anything! You could just sit around and feel lethargic. It was a reward for all the hurrying and hard work.

M: What's this about hard work?

EP: What do you mean?

M: You mentioned hard work.

EP: Well, that's what everyone *did*—at least most of the time. My father worked hard all his life. My mother worked hard at home. But on vacations everyone got to sit around and do nothing. We all felt lethargic.

M: It was better than hurrying and hard work?

EP: Oh yes! It was the *opposite* of hard work. Hard work was stressful, or painful. It was a constant burden. Feeling lethargic was *good*. It's what you got to do *after* the hard work.

M: So. When you recently decided to stop hurrying, did you decide to reward yourself by feeling lethargic?

EP: Huh?

M: You heard.

EP: Did I decide to *reward* myself?

M: Yes.

EP: Gee. I don't know . . .

M: If feeling lethargic was a reward for you in your past—the reward for all the hurrying you did—it would make sense for you to start feeling it now, right after you decided to stop hurrying.

EP: (Eyes lighting up) Boy! I really think you've hit on something. Actually, now that I think of it, I really feel lethargic quite often. Whenever I do anything my Parent says I should do, I usually feel lethargic afterward. It's like a reward for doing what I was told. Sometimes the lethargy is hard to get rid of. When I feel lethargic, I don't think very clearly. Also, my mind sort of goes blank.

M: Is *that* a reward, too—not having to think?

EP: Yes it is. It goes along with the lethargy—not having to *do* anything, and not having to *think* about anything! That's why it's such a hindrance to me now. I've been wanting to start thinking for some time, and the lethargy's been getting in my way.

M: Now we're getting somewhere!

EP: Oh!! I just thought of something else! I think I decided once that if I ever had to choose between lethargy and hard work, I'd choose lethargy. I decided that working hard was dumb, that it was much better to feel lethargic.

M: That's very interesting.

EP: Yes. (Earnestly) I also think at some level I've been feeling that this process we've been going through is too much work. I think I've been tricking myself into feeling lethargic as a reward for going through all this frustration!

M: You're really getting clear now. Do you want to stop rewarding yourself this way?

EP: Yes!

M: *Will* you?

EP: Yes! I sure will! Now that I know this feeling is just an old reward, it's a lot easier for me to deal with. I can stop feeling it, and reward myself in other ways!

M: Good. Now, before we leave the subject, can you tell me whether this lethargy—or boredom, as you first called it—was an Adapted Child feeling or a Natural Child feeling?

EP: It was an Adapted Child feeling. It was programmed. I learned it on my early vacations at the lake.

M: And what have you decided to do about it?

EP: I've decided to stop feeling it, to turn the tape off.

M: And *how* have you been able to do this?

EP: Well, it's kind of hard to explain, but by going back and remembering how I first started feeling lethargic, I can understand the decision I made about when and how to feel it, and I can decide not to do it anymore.

M: Okay! *That's* how you turn off your tapes! You've done it several times now, and I want to keep calling your attention to it, so that you can continue to get a feel for the process.

EP: That's fine by me. I appreciate it.

Comments

1. You can't become rich if you don't have the energy to do what you want. You need *energy* to rearrange your life! You need to feel eager, excited, and enthusiastic! If you *don't* (that is, if you feel bored, sad, depressed, listless, apathetic, exhausted, confused, worried, distracted, melancholy, or defeated, instead), you must first redecide such feelings before you can get on with the business of making money or becoming happy.

Energy is something you feel! (A feeling, in its simplest form, is energy that is focused in a certain direction, at a certain intensity, and with a certain intent.) If your energy is directed inwardly (as when you feel depressed or defeated), or randomly (as when you feel confused or distracted), or if it's kept at a low level (as when you feel bored or listless), or even at a high level but focused unproductively (as when you feel angry at someone in a vengeful way), you're not using your energy to succeed. You're using it to *stop* yourself from succeeding!

Learning to alter your energy usage involves learning to redecide what you've learned to feel. It involves replacing your old low-energy feelings with new higher-energy feelings. (You can't feel enthusiastic and depressed simultaneously, and if you feel depressed, you won't have the energy to get what you want.)

2. If you've found a low-energy feeling you want to get rid of (like EP's lethargy), and if you can't identify its related justifications and Parent driver, you might try thinking back to see if you can locate the situation where you first started having the feeling. (It may take some practice, but most people *can* learn to jog their memory sufficiently to come up with the origins of most of their key feelings.) The history of how you learned to feel is the history of how you learned to use your energy. By reviewing your past, you can learn about your decisions to feel certain feelings (like EP's feeling lethargy as a reward), which might never surface in any other way.

3. All people have the same general ability to produce high-level, well-focused energy. Their metabolism rates may differ slightly, and they may have different high and low points during the day, but unless their diets are substantially lacking in nutrients or their breathing is so shallow that enough oxygen doesn't get into their bloodstream, people *do* have the capacity to feel genuinely eager and excited most of the day. Whether they do or not depends less on physical or chemical factors than on what they've learned to feel (or, more accurately, on how they've learned to direct their energy).*

4. As you learn how you focus your energy, watch how often you focus it inwardly, in a dialogue with your Parent. Watch how you use your energy to *resist* the demands of your Parent (and feel guilty, worried, or jumpy). Watch how your *Parent* uses it to stop you from doing things (and you then feel restless, discontented, unsettled, and uneasy). Watch what happens when your Parent *wins* the battle (and you end up feeling indifferent, listless, apathetic, and defeated). Consider what might happen if you didn't use your energy in these ways, if you freed it for use in achieving your real goals in life.

---

*Chronic tension in a person's muscles, reflected in stooped posture or an unusually tight body, is one exception to this statement. It may *physically* prevent oxygen from reaching all parts of the body, including the brain. This will be discussed in Chapter 17.

CHAPTER TEN

Learning
How to Learn

EP: I've been reading some books on how to get rich!

M: Are they working?

EP: What do you mean?

M: Are you getting rich from reading these books?

EP: Of course not! I'm not getting rich *myself!* I'm *reading* about how to get rich!

M: Oh. When are you going to stop reading about it and start *doing* it?

EP: What do you mean by that?

M: You said before that you wanted to get rich. Did you decide to get rich, or did you decide just to read about getting rich?

EP: Well, before I can get rich, I have to learn how!

M: Do you think you can learn by reading?

EP: Naturally! That's why I'm doing it!

M: Very few people have ever gotten rich from reading books.

EP: What are you talking about? There are dozens of books out, and all the guys who wrote them got rich!

M: And how many of the people *reading* these books have gotten rich?

EP: I don't know . . .

M: Millions?

EP: No. I doubt it.

M: Hundreds of thousands?

EP: I doubt that, too.

M: Do you think there are tens of thousands?

EP: Probably not. I guess . . . maybe hundreds.

M: Do *you* know anyone who's gotten rich from reading books?

EP: No, I don't.

M: Then why are you reading books?

EP: I thought I was reading them to learn how to get rich. Now I'm not so sure. I hear you saying it won't do me any good.

M: What made you think you could get rich from reading books?

EP: I don't know. I have to learn somehow!

M: Yes. But why turn to reading?

EP: I guess because it's the only way I know how to learn. I don't know any other way.

M: Do you think most rich people learned to get rich from reading books?

EP: Now that you mention it, probably not. But how *did* they learn?

M: From experience.

EP: What do you mean?

M: The best way to learn is from experience.

EP: But that's why I got the books! To find out about the *experiences* of people who've already *gotten* rich!

M: They're the ones who experienced getting rich. What you're experiencing is reading about it. The two experiences are different.

EP: How are they different?

M: *Your* experience will enable you to become a good source of information about how other people got rich. However, *their* experience enabled them to get rich.

EP: But how can I learn what they've done if I don't read about it?

M: You don't need to know what they've done. You only

need to know the process they used, and you already *know* that.

EP: I already know the process?

M: Sure! Don't you remember? It involves deciding what you want to do, and then making sure that what you're presently doing isn't preventing you from doing what you want.

EP: Hmmm. But why do all these people write books on how to get rich if no one really needs to know what they've done?

M: They believe they can share their experience through words. But they can't. Words only communicate information—and you don't need any more information. You need to focus on yourself.

EP: I remember you said the same thing a while back —that I don't need any more information. You said that what I needed instead of more information was to learn more about what I feel.

M: Yes. Feelings are something you experience. Information is something you process in your head. It's not an experience at all. There's a big difference.

EP: But how will knowing what I feel help me get rich?

M: It will help you identify how you're *preventing* yourself from getting rich.

EP: Damn! You said that before, too. I still don't understand.

M: If you feel bad, you can't concentrate on getting rich. You're too distracted. You can't find the Natural Child energy you need. However, if you *know* you feel bad, you can do something about it. If the part of you feeling bad is your Natural Child, responding spontaneously to your immediate environment, you can change that environment—you can make yourself more comfortable where you are, or move to better surroundings. If the part of you feeling bad is your Adapted Child, you can turn off the tape and feel good.

EP: I think I'm finally catching on. If my immediate physical environment is comfortable, I have no need to feel bad. Therefore, if I'm still not feeling good, I'll know this feeling is in my Adapted Child, and that it has to do with something from my past. I'll also know that my Parent is probably saying something to me to trigger the feeling. And *that's* the first thing to work on before doing anything else about getting rich.

M: That's it!

EP: Well, it sort of makes sense to me, but it seems awfully roundabout.

M: That's the only way it works.

EP: What about the actual *experience* of getting rich, as opposed to the experience of reading about it. How do I get *that,* and what do I feel as I'm experiencing it?

M: How do you want to get rich?

EP: What do you mean?

M: You can get rich any way you want. Which way would you like to choose?

EP: I can get rich *any way* I *want?!*

M: Yes. (Pause) What are you feeling right now?

EP: I'm confused.

M: Confused is not a feeling. Confusion is a way of hiding from what is real.

EP: Huh?

M: (Looks directly at EP, but doesn't speak)

EP: (Weakly) I'm hiding from what's real?

M: Yes.

EP: What's the reality that I'm hiding from?

M: That you can get rich any way you want.

EP: But I don't know *how* to get rich!

M: That's your Adapted Child speaking.

EP: No it's not. It's my Adult!

M: There may be an Adult component to your statement, but what I heard was your Adapted Child.

EP: What makes you say that?

M: I *heard* it. But in addition, it's a stock Adapted Child response. Little children are always saying "I don't know" and "I don't know how" when big people ask them things. They're afraid of being punished. You've been programmed to say that for years. (Speaking casually) How are you preventing yourself from deciding how you want to get rich?

EP: (Defensively) What do you mean, "preventing myself"?

M: You know.

EP: (Even more defensively) Wait just a minute now. You're taking a lot for granted. You're really beginning to push me!

M: It's a favor.

EP: (Explosively) What?! Pushing me is a *favor*?

M: Yes. It's like the gift I gave you earlier. I don't *have* to push you. Consider it a gift.

EP: Hmmm. (Thinking deeply) What did you ask me?

M: What you're doing to prevent yourself from deciding how you want to get rich.

EP: I really can't say I know.

M: What are you feeling right now?

EP: I'm confused again. Hiding from something, I guess . . .

M: How does it serve you to stay confused?

EP: How does it *serve* me?

M: Yes. What are you getting out of staying confused that makes you do it so automatically?

EP: Well . . . I guess one thing is I don't have to acknowledge your statement is correct. I don't have to believe it! And if I stay confused, I can avoid being clear enough to know what you're saying is true!

M: And why do you want to do that?

EP: Because if I acknowledged it was true, it would be very scary!

M: You'd scare yourself?

EP: Yes.

M: What's that about?

EP: It means I'd have to look at a lot of things around me—things I've used to *justify* staying poor—and I'd have to do something about them. I can't acknowledge your statement and still keep things the same in my life.

M: That awareness is worth holding on to. Stay with it for a moment. That's what you're doing to prevent yourself from deciding to get rich.

EP: (Pause) I see what you mean. I'm trying to hold on to my past. I don't want to give it up. I don't want to go into the future!

M: You don't want to *change* and go into the future. You'd prefer to get rich without doing anything differently, and without seeing any more clearly than you do right now. You'd prefer to go into the future *that* way. But you can't, and still get rich. It's impossible. Your present level of awareness and your present way of doing things have led to the mess you're in. If you continue with them, you'll remain poor and unhappy.

EP: Do all people who get rich experience this pull between the past and the future, between confusion and clarity?

M: Yes. It's called fear.

EP: How do they get rid of it?

M: There are two ways to get rid of it. You can stop wanting to get rich, or wanting to change anything else in your life, and you'll no longer push yourself to the point of fear. The fear itself will disappear. Or you can examine how you scare yourself and decide to stop doing it.

EP: And people who get rich choose the second way?

M: They first decide they want to get rich, and then examine how they prevent themselves from doing so. One of the first things they discover is they've been scaring themselves. Then they stop it.

EP: How do *I* scare myself?

M: *You* tell *me*.

EP: (Pondering for a moment) Well, I keep thinking my past is more important to me than my future. I keep thinking I'll lose everything I have—all my money, all my friends, my skills, and everything else of value to me. I keep thinking everyone will desert me, and I won't have any way to cope.

M: How does it serve you to keep thinking these thoughts?

EP: It delays my moment of clarity. (Eyes lighting up) Wow! That's an important insight. I scare myself in order to delay my moment of clarity; and by delaying my moment of clarity, I continue to scare myself. It's a vicious cycle!

M: Very good! You're getting clear again.

EP: But why would I do that?

M: You tell me!

EP: Hmmm. (Pause) Well . . . I guess that's how I keep this fear circulating around inside myself. That's how I sustain the feeling!

M: Good. Now, do you want to continue doing it?

EP: No! Damn it! I certainly don't!

M: Then tell me how you'd like to get rich.

EP: Okay. I'd like to get rich by doing something I won't have to work hard at. I'd like to find a way to get rich and still have a lot of free time. I'd also like to travel a lot.

M: Good. Anything else?

EP: This sounds crazy!

M: That's your Parent, interfering with our conversation. I'm not talking to your Parent. . . . Now, please tell me more about how you'd like to get rich.

EP: Well, I'd like to be able to make my own hours, and not have to do anything I don't want to do. And, I'd like it to be fun.

M: So far, you've told me in several different ways you don't want to have your Parent involved—you want to do it from your Natural Child.

EP: Huh? (Pause) That's really interesting! I did say that, didn't I?

M: How could you arrange to get rich without having your Parent involved?

EP: I could just get rid of my Parent. If I turned off all the tapes I don't like, my Parent wouldn't tell me I have to do anything. I could decide for myself what I wanted to do.

M: Fine. Now, how can your Natural Child come up with some way for you to get rich?

EP: I guess it just has to start looking for things that might be fun.

M: Okay. Do you think you can do that?

EP: (*Very* enthusiastically) Yes! I sure can! It sounds exciting!

M: Are you scaring yourself now?

EP: No, I'm not.

M: How did you *stop* scaring yourself?

EP: I started thinking about having fun and getting rich at the same time!

M: *Now* you've started to learn! *This* way is much more useful than looking for information in books.

Comments

1. Few people are lucky enough to actually learn how to learn. For most of us, learning is a hit-or-miss process with little or no logic behind it. We're *taught* that it involves collecting facts and acquiring specific skills for specific tasks, but once we've obtained those facts and skills, we often find something's missing.

Our really important learning occurs outside the formal process we've been taught. Our most crucial lessons come through experiencing something rather than being told about it. Real learning occurs when we're assimilating, and using, the facts and skills we've learned—not when we're merely learning about them. But our lessons in growing up rarely mention this. In fact, we're usually encouraged *not* to experience things on our own. We're told not to experiment, not to try things out, and not to look foolish. If we're not physically restrained, we're either punished forcefully enough, or made to feel embarrassed enough, to discourage us from continuing any further.

2. There's only one way you can learn to experience becoming rich and happy, and that's to just start experiencing it! It takes *action* on your part! If you haven't started taking such action already, you need to seriously consider making some new decisions on how you plan to *learn!* You can't learn to get rich or become happy by reading this or any other book!

If you haven't started yet, here are some questions to ask yourself:

(a) How do I plan to learn to become rich and happy? (By collecting facts, by learning from experience, or both?)

(b) What method of learning am I presently using (as reflected in my present actions)?

(c) What could I do now that I'm not already doing to help myself learn from experience?

3. Learning from experience involves knowing what you want, assessing the implications of your future actions to obtain what you want, weighing the possible consequences, and, once you've prepared yourself as best you can, simply taking the plunge! If it works, it works; and if it doesn't work, you can learn from it. (That's what learning from experience is all about!)

One possible consequence of your future actions (usually the scariest) is that you might lose something you don't want to give up (family, friends, possessions, security, or self-esteem). While there's no way to totally protect yourself from this possibility, you can prepare yourself for it *by being willing to risk giving up everything you have!* (Being willing to give something up doesn't mean you'll necessarily lose it. It only means you'll be prepared to lose it, if you have to.)

There may be times when you feel you have *everything* at risk, and that only a fool would prepare himself to lose it willingly. Yet unless your *life itself* is at stake, you'll rarely be risking something you can't replace. You can always regain your self-esteem. You'll always have time ahead of you —time to make more money, time to remarry, and time to get another job. The only thing you won't be able to replace is your past. (You won't be able to do it all again in exactly the same way you did before.) Learning to give up your past is one of the most difficult tasks you'll be faced with.

4. The key decision in deciding to learn from experience *is to decide to act on the basis of what you want.* You can't get experience if you don't take action, and the clearest way to

take action is to do what you want. In making your decisions, you might want to ask yourself:

(a) What is there in my present life I want, that I'm willing to act on to obtain?

(b) What is there I *don't* want anymore, that I'm willing to act on to get rid of?

(c) What am I afraid to lose if I go ahead and act?

(d) What would life be like if I *did lose it*?

(e) What decision must I make in order to become willing to give it up?

(f) Am I willing to try some new things just to find out what happens?

(g) What would it be like if I tried something and it worked? (Would I be scared, or happy?)

(h) What would be so bad if I failed?

CHAPTER
ELEVEN

The Obstacles
to Power

EP: Martian?

M: Yes.

EP: After I stop scaring myself—entirely, that is—will it be easy for me to get rich?

M: As easy as you want to make it.

EP: No. I didn't mean it that way. (Mildly frustrated) I guess I meant to make a statement . . . . I'm wondering if fear is my only obstacle to getting rich.

M: Fear isn't an obstacle. Fear is a way of using energy.

EP: Then what *is* my present obstacle, if it isn't fear?

M: Confusion.

EP: You mean the confusions and fantasies I carry around with me?

M: Yes. And the decisions you've made about your life that are based on them.

EP: Okay. But when I stop scaring myself, I'll be able to redecide those decisions, and I'll give up my confusions and fantasies, right?

M: Yes. You'll trade your confusions in for clarity. You've already started doing it.

EP: Okay. What I want to know is, once I achieve clarity, will I be able to get rich fairly easily?

M: No. You'll become clear. But clarity, by itself, doesn't bring riches.

EP: That's what I was afraid of. Are there other obstacles?

M: Yes, there's another that will emerge just as soon as you've traded in your confusions.

EP: What will it be?

M: Clarity.

EP: (Very puzzled) Clarity? How can clarity be an obstacle? I thought clarity was my goal!

M: Clarity is your goal, now, but it won't be your goal once you've achieved it. It will become something you *have,* and you'll be afraid to give it up. You'll be afraid to lose it.

EP: But how will it become an obstacle to me?

M: You'll use your clarity to hide behind, just as you used your confusions to hide from clarity.

EP: I don't see how I could possibly lose my clarity, once I've achieved it.

M: You'll have to *use* your clarity if you want to get rich. And once you start using it, you'll be afraid of losing it.

EP: I don't understand.

M: It will take energy for you to use your clarity, but it will also take energy for you to remain clear. As you start using your energy to get rich, you'll experience an energy drain. You'll begin to scare yourself. You'll be afraid that in the effort to get rich you'll have to do things that will make you lose your clarity.

EP: You mean that I'll think I won't have enough energy to both *use* my clarity and *maintain* it at the same time; so I'll back off, thinking it's more important to maintain it?

M: Right.

EP: *Will* I have enough energy?

M: If you want to find it, it will be there.

EP: Where will I find it?

M: In your fear.

EP: Oh! You mean that I'll be using energy to scare myself, and that instead of scaring myself I could use that energy to push myself forward?

M: In a sense. But rather than pushing yourself forward,

you'll merely need to stop holding yourself back. Your Natural Child will move forward on its own momentum.

EP: I think I see what you mean. (Pause) You said earlier that I'd be hiding behind my clarity—that I'd be hiding *from* something. What will I be hiding from?

M: Power.

EP: Power? What kind of power?

M: Power! The power to get whatever you want by using your clarity. Just as you were comfortable with your confusions, you'll become comfortable with your clarity. You'll be afraid to move forward toward power.

EP: So, I'll be afraid all over again.

M: Yes. Fear always comes back. Even after you become powerful and make money easily and become very happy, your fear will come back.

EP: It will?

M: Without fail.

EP: What could I possibly be afraid of once I'm rich and powerful?

M: *Losing* your money and power. But you can make use of your fear. Rather than use it to hide behind, or to protect yourself, you can turn it into productive energy and move forward some more.

EP: Move forward some more? Where else is there to go?

M: Ask any rich person.

EP: When does it all end?

M: Power is your last obstacle. It ends when you've overcome your need for power.

EP: And when is that?

M: When you're willing to give up your power. When you no longer need to protect it.

EP: Where will I be then?

M: You will be fully matured as an Earth Person.

Comments

1. Do you remember the last time you climbed a ladder? Do you remember the exertion of going from one step to

the next? Do you remember feeling fine when you stood with both feet on the same rung, but then feeling a bit off balance as you moved one foot off that rung to step up to the next? Do you remember moving with much less confidence as you neared the top? And do you remember wondering, at some point near the top—with one foot on one rung and one foot on the next, but not balancing comfortably on either—whether it wouldn't be better to just cling to the ladder and inch your way down?

At that critical moment near the top, off balance and in between rungs, were you more interested in gaining the rung above, or more afraid of losing the rung below?

That's the question EP's faced with. He's got one foot on clarity and the other foot on the rung above—the rung of power. He's beginning to cling to the ladder and look down. Yet the only way he can gain the rung above is to give up the rung below.

CHAPTER
TWELVE

Separating Yourself
from the World

EP: Martian, I'm worried.

M: How does worrying serve you?

EP: No, seriously. I'm really worried.

M: And I'm interested in knowing what you're getting out of it.

EP: I don't mean it that way! I'm really *bothered* about something! Can't I just talk for a while without your getting into that "how does it serve me" business?

M: Okay. Go ahead.

EP: Well, I went home yesterday and told my family that we're moving to smaller quarters so that we can save some money. (Pause) I'm going to pay off my debts and build up a little cash. If I'm going to have the freedom to do what I want, I'll need to have some money.

M: That sounds like progress. What's the problem?

EP: Well, we're not exactly living on Park Avenue right now, and the whole family complained. They just don't like the idea of cutting back to save money.

M: That's *their* problem, not yours.

EP: Well, they can *make* it my problem!

M: How?

EP: By complaining a lot! It *becomes* my problem when they complain so much they make my life miserable!

M: No. It doesn't become your problem. It's still *their* problem. Their *complaining* is your problem.

EP: So? What's the difference?

M: There's a big difference! Your action involved an important decision on your part. It certainly isn't a problem. It's a point of clarity! The fact that it might create problems for other people is something for *them* to deal with, not you.

EP: Well, they're dealing with it all right. That's what's bothering me. They're complaining an awful lot!

M: Okay. And as I said, the *complaining* is your problem. The question now is how you plan to deal with it.

EP: That's why I'm so worried.

M: Oh?

EP: Yes! I'm afraid they won't go along with me.

M: So?

EP: What do you mean, "So"? That's what my problem *really* is! I'm afraid they won't go along with me!

M: Okay. That's clear. (Pause) How does it serve you?

EP: How does what serve me?

M: Your fear.

EP: (Face flushing) Wait a minute! My problem is my *family!* It's not my fear!

M: No. You were right the first time. You said you were *afraid* they wouldn't go along with you. Your problem is fear. Stick with it now and you'll learn something.

EP: Okay.

M: How does your fear serve you?

EP: Well . . . (Thinking seriously) It keeps me worried. It keeps me uptight.

M: And how does it serve you to stay worried?

EP: (Pausing thoughtfully) It enables me to stop myself. It enables me to decide to change my mind—to stop myself from just going ahead and doing what I want.

M: Do you want to do that?

EP: No.

M: Okay, then. How do you get into it? How do you set up the worry and the fear?

EP: I hear them complain, and I start thinking that they won't go along with me—because that's what they're saying! They're saying they won't go along!

M: And?

EP: And I think that if they won't go along, I'll have to back down.

M: Why is that?

EP: Because they're my family. I shouldn't be the source of all their problems, and I certainly don't want to cause a breakup!

M: Okay. And how do you scare yourself?

EP: Well, right at this point I start becoming afraid I won't get what I want.

M: And do you remember what I said fear was?

EP: Yes. You said fear was using energy to stop myself.

M: Do you see the connection?

EP: What? (Deep silence) Oh . . . wow! That's horrible! As soon as I become afraid I won't get what I want, I *automatically* start using my energy to stop myself; because that's what fear is—using energy to stop myself! God! It's almost a *guarantee* that I won't get what I want!

M: Very good.

EP: That's really fascinating!

M: I know. Now here's what I've heard so far. Here's what happens between you and your family. First of all, you make a decision about what you want to do, and it creates problems for those around you. Second, they respond by complaining. Their hope, consciously or not, is to manipulate you into reversing your decision. Third, you respond to their complaining by worrying. You don't ignore them, you don't get angry, and you don't do any one of a number of other things you might do. You worry.

EP: That's pretty much what happens.

M: Your Natural Child makes your initial decision—the decision to move to smaller quarters—but doesn't say anything further in response to their complaints. You respond to their complaints from your Parent, by saying you shouldn't be a source of difficulty to your family, and from your Adapted Child, by scaring yourself by fantasizing about a breakup.

EP: Yeah. You're right. That's just what happens. It just proves that my Parent and Adapted Child are programmed, that they're on tape. That's what I *always* do when my family complains.

M: Would you like to see what the other parts of you have to say about all this?

EP: I sure would!

M: Okay. Let's do it, then. What does your Natural Child have to say about all the complaints?

EP: It says that I still want to conserve cash and get some economic freedom, regardless of what *they* say!

M: And your Adult?

EP: Well, my Adult says that there isn't much sense talking to my family from my Natural Child. I already told them what I wanted, and they didn't hear. They're really not interested in what I want.

M: What does your Adult say about their complaining?

EP: It says they do it all the time.

M: What else?

EP: It says that's how they keep getting what they want; at least that's how they keep getting what they want from me!

M: Okay. How does your Adult tell you to respond to their complaining?

EP: It says . . . (Pause) That's a hard one. It says that worrying won't help, but it doesn't say what else to do. My Adult doesn't have any information on how they'd respond if I didn't worry, or if I ignored them. It's never happened.

M: I didn't ask your Adult how they'd respond if you didn't worry. I asked about *your* response to their complaints.

EP: It doesn't *say* how to respond.

M: Suppose you told it that you wanted to move to smaller quarters. How would it say to do that?

EP: It would say for me just to move.

M: And how would you describe your action to your family?

EP: I'd say, "I'm moving."

M: Oh. That sounds simple enough. Will you do it?

EP: Well, I'd like to, but I can't—not if it causes a breakup.

M: You *can*. What you're saying is you *won't*. Please take responsibility for your own actions.

EP: (Looking up, startled) What?

M: You said that you *can't* move, as if there were some external force preventing you, and you weren't responsible for your inaction. But there *is* no external force. You can move if you want to. You make your own decisions about what you do. If you decide not to move, the way to express it is to say that you *won't* move, not that you can't.

EP: Oh. I see what you mean. Okay. I *won't* move if it causes a breakup.

M: Now we're back to the problem of your Adapted Child. Why are you afraid of breaking up the family?

EP: Well, first of all, you just shouldn't get divorced. It's against my religion, and besides that, it's a sign of failure.

M: Failure?

EP: Yes. If you get divorced, you've failed in your marriage. You've screwed it up. It's obvious to everyone, but worst of all, it's obvious to yourself. You just didn't succeed at it.

M: What's this about failure and success?

EP: What do you mean?

M: You're measuring, or judging, your marriage. I was wondering what that's about.

EP: Well, a marriage that lasts is a success. A marriage that doesn't last is a failure.

M: What about happiness? Is an unhappy marriage that lasts still a success—just because it lasts?

EP: No. Of course not. But even if a marriage isn't always happy, it's better for the couple to try to hold it together than to get a divorce. At least they kept trying.

M: Where is the virtue in trying?

EP: It means you haven't given up.

M: So?

EP: If you give up, it means you're a failure.

M: Are you aware that it's your Parent saying all these things about failure and success—about how you *shouldn't* get divorced?

EP: My Parent?

M: Yes. Your Parent's judging you. It's saying when you're a failure. It's saying that you shouldn't give up—you shouldn't get divorced, or you'll be a failure.

EP: Are you saying people *should* get divorced?

M: No. I'm not saying anything about what people should or should not do. I'm saying that I hear your Parent explaining your behavior to me—telling me how it stops you from doing what you want.

EP: Oh . . .

M: What would happen if you broke up your marriage?

EP: I couldn't live with myself.

M: What's that about?

EP: I'd know that I failed!

M: You mean your Parent would beat on you?

EP: Yes. That's one way of putting it.

M: You'd be able to live with yourself if you got your Parent off your back, wouldn't you?

EP: Hmmm. I never thought of it that way.

M: Suppose you just decided to do what you want, and you let your wife take care of any divorce decisions. Would you consider yourself responsible for the breakup?

EP: No. Not if I wasn't being selfish. But this latest decision to move is pure selfishness!

M: Do you hear your Parent again?

EP: What? Saying I'm selfish?

M: Yes.

EP: But I *am!* At least that's what you've been suggesting, and I've been going along with it. "Do what you want," you say, and that's selfish—particularly when it hurts other people.

M: That's what your Parent says about what I suggest. I have no interest in what your Parent says. Your Parent is a bunch of tapes. It doesn't see or hear! It doesn't see the results of what it makes you do! You've been doing what it said you should do most of your life, and look where it's gotten you! You can continue doing so, if you like. The choice is yours.

EP: But if I disregard all the things I know I *should* do, I'll be lost. I won't have any guidelines. And if I stick to my guns about this decision to move, and disregard all the things my Parent says about being self-centered and thoughtless, I really *could* end up divorced!

M: So?

EP: Then I'd be all alone. I'd be all by myself.

M: And?

EP: It would be awfully lonely . . .

M: Ah. That's what you're afraid of. That's why your Adapted Child won't budge. You're afraid of being lonely.

EP: (Thinking deeply) When you get right down to it, I guess that's it. And it would be hard to find someone else. It was hard enough to find someone who'd marry me the first time around!

M: You *imagine* it will be hard. Actually, once you start making decisions for yourself, and once you start disregarding your old programming, you'll have a lot more to offer. Few people can do this. It's a rare skill. You'll also have a lot more to offer your *present* family. Their response to such decisiveness might surprise you.

EP: But in order to become decisive, I have to risk being lonely, don't I?

M: Lonely is a feeling. It's different from the condition of being alone. It's a feeling in your Adapted Child, and you need not feel it. You can be alone without feeling lonely. You can be alone and feel comfortable.

EP: You mean I've been going through all this just to avoid a feeling?!

M: Yes. It's the problem you have with *all* your Adapted

Child feelings. You think you have to feel them, so you avoid them. It was the same with guilt. Don't you remember?

EP: I sure do. It's amazing that my avoidance can be so strong, though.

M: Yes. Apparently you'd prefer being with people who manipulate you against your will to get what they want, to being alone and risking feeling lonely.

EP: It really sounds foolish when you put it that way. (Pause) How can I stop the feeling of loneliness?

M: How do you *start* it?

EP: I don't know. I usually try so hard to avoid it that I don't know how it feels.

M: Then fantasize about it. Think about being all by yourself—after your family has left you. See yourself all alone in a little room. Try to induce the feeling.

EP: Hmmm . . . okay. (Pause)

M: Are you doing it?

EP: Yes. But it's hard. It's such an uncomfortable feeling.

M: Stick with it.

EP: I'm thinking that nobody likes me. That nobody cares about me. That nobody wants to be with me. I'm thinking that I must be a nothing sort of person because nobody wants to be around me.

M: Very good. Stay with it.

EP: I'm thinking that I'm helpless. I'm in this room all by myself, and I can't get anybody to speak to me. I can't get anybody even to come in and visit. I'm really such a zero that no one wants to come in and visit me.

M: Okay. Is that what it feels like to feel lonely?

EP: Yes. It's awful!

M: How are you inducing the feeling?

EP: I'm saying these terrible things about myself. I'm in my Parent, saying that I'm worthless. And I'm getting the feeling that people are leaving me, trying to get away from me, as if I'm a leper or something.

M: Do you want the people to leave?

EP: No! I want them to stay! But they won't. They don't

care anything about me. They're just leaving, and on the way out, they're saying things like "Why would anyone want to be with such a miserable nothing person."

M: Very good. Can you describe the essence of your feeling?

EP: Yes. It's as if I'm losing something. There's nothing I can do to stop these people from leaving me. They see so little in me that there's absolutely nothing I can do to change their minds.

M: You want them to come back and you're powerless to do anything about it.

EP: Yes. There's no way I can stop it. That's what it is! I really feel powerless!

M: It's a terrible feeling?

EP: It certainly is. I'm shuddering just thinking about it.

M: Stick with this fantasy. As you sit there, in this little room, what can you do to start feeling powerful, and how can you exercise your power?

EP: (Pause) I don't know. Everyone's gone by now. There's nothing left for me to do.

M: Do you have to sit there and dwell on it?

EP: Hmmm. No. I guess not. But I can't think of. . . . Oh! Wait a minute! I've got it! (Eyes lighting up)

M: Yes?

EP: I can just get up and walk out of the room! I don't have to stay there!

M: Good. And as you start walking out, as you start moving, do you begin feeling powerful?

EP: Yes, I do. I was only feeling powerless as I sat there and concentrated on those people, and on not being able to influence them.

M: Okay. Do you feel lonely, now?

EP: No. I feel fine.

M: That's really good. What we've just learned is how you induce the feeling of loneliness you've tried so often to avoid. It's an early feeling in your life—one that comes whenever you imagine people leaving you without your permission—whenever you imagine people who are beyond your control just getting up and leaving. Something like that probably happened once when you were young, and the feeling that devastated you at the time went on tape and locked itself in your memory.

EP: That's fascinating!

M: The way to get rid of the feeling is to recognize that you *are* powerless to control other people, but you're not powerless to control yourself. You don't have to sit there and take it. At least, not anymore, you don't. You can get up and just leave.

EP: (Excitedly) Wow! I think I've just decided to move to smaller quarters, regardless of what my family thinks. I don't *have* to be afraid of feeling lonely!

M: You *think* you've decided?

EP: I've *decided!*

M: And this won't create an unreasonable hardship on your family?

EP: No. They might not *like* it, but it's not something they can't live with, if they want to.

M: Good. Now, can you tell me how you did all this?

EP: Well, I stopped my Adapted Child from controlling me. In order to do that, I first got my Parent off my back. I stopped it from giving all the surface reasons why I shouldn't do what I want—shouldn't cause problems, shouldn't fail, and all that. Then I got to the real reason I was stopping myself. I was afraid to feel lonely. I re-created the feeling of loneliness—I really got with it and induced the feeling in myself to find out exactly how I did it, and then all of a sudden it didn't have any more power over me.

M: Very good. Now there's one last thing to remember—something that will help you in many future situations.

EP: Okay. What is it?

M: Powerlessness. It's your fear of powerlessness.

EP: What do you mean?

M: Whenever you stop yourself from doing what you want, there's an Adapted Child feeling you're trying to avoid. Under each Adapted Child feeling you try to avoid, there's a more basic feeling of powerlessness. It's the source of all your fear. It's the ultimate feeling all Earth People avoid.

EP: It's the opposite of *powerful!*

M: Yes. And the important insight is that the way to overcome *all* the Adapted Child feelings you don't like is to discover the powerless component in them, and simply do away with it by finding a way to be powerful in each situation.

EP: And this works for *all* situations?

M: Absolutely.

EP: Wow! This is almost the ultimate secret!

M: It is for Earth People. There's nothing more important to know on Earth. If you use it carefully, you can have everything you want.

Comments

1. Of all the things we risk when we decide to operate on the basis of what we want, nothing is more important to us, nor given up more reluctantly, than our feelings from our past. When the chips are down, the ideas and feelings we've collected along the way (and stored in our Parent and Adapted Child) usually mean more to us than all our more obvious material assets combined.

In this chapter EP is much less concerned about risking his marriage than he is about risking feeling lonely. In your own life you'll consistently find that the reasons you hold yourself back are *not* the surface reasons you normally speak of, but rather your fear of feeling lonely, rejected, ignored, abandoned, empty, helpless, embarrassed, foolish, vulnerable, or some other Adapted Child feeling most people try to avoid. This will hold true no matter how strong, healthy, or free from "hang-ups" you may be! You may not normally *feel* these feelings because you've arranged your life to avoid them, but you are programmed to feel them if you ever change your behavior.

All of us manipulate ourselves, and *stop* ourselves from acting, by using our Adapted Child feelings. The way to identify these feelings for yourself is to sort through all your usual justifications and rationales until you know what it is you *don't want to feel* if you risk changing your behavior.

2. In previous chapters we discussed three methods of identifying the Parent driver you might be using to induce certain Adapted Child feelings. They were: listening for the driver and trying to spot the Parent words in actual conversation ("hurry up," for example); inferring what the driver might be from observing your own behavior; and trying to recall an early scene in which you first felt these feelings, and identifying how you might have learned to feel them, and what automatic things your Parent might be telling you to do (e.g., feeling lethargic as a reward). This chapter describes a fourth method—that of fantasizing, or "making up," a typical situation in which you feel these Adapted Child feelings with particularly strong intensity, and examining all aspects of the scene (what people are there, what they're saying, what they're doing, what you're feeling, etc.). Surprisingly, this method often works even better than the others! Our fantasies often combine key elements of several real-life situations which we would otherwise never think to associate, resulting in a more efficient method of getting to the core of the problem. *Try* it whenever you're stumped!

3. The powerless component in our Adapted Child feelings that stop us from doing what we want is particularly useful to know about. The issue of power is extremely important to us in growing up. In situations where we can handle ourselves comfortably, take effective action, and get what we want, we *have the power to act*, and we record feelings of power (confidence, enthusiasm, self-satisfaction, and the like). In other situations the reverse is true. When we *don't* handle ourselves comfortably, when there's *no* action we know of to take, and when we simply *can't* get what we want, we record feelings of powerlessness (we feel helpless, victimized, intimidated, frustrated, trapped, persecuted, or

something similar). Later in life (often in situations where we're once again trying to get what we want) these feelings replay in our minds and we trap ourselves into further inaction. Underneath all these feelings is the paralyzing effect of the *real powerlessness we once felt!*

Often by merely recognizing this, and then by *doing* something—either in fantasy or in real life—that we actually have the power to do (walk away, start to talk, change the subject, etc.), we can regain the feeling of power we once lost.

4. This chapter deals heavily with family relationships and how EP allows them to influence his behavior. This influence occurs largely because EP's Parent ideas and Adapted Child feelings are reinforced by the attitudes of those around him. Rather than help him do what he wants, the people closest to him try to stop him. They, too, operate from their own feelings of powerlessness, and by trying to get him to do what *they* want (rather than what *he* wants), they avoid dealing with the grief or pain they fear might surface within themselves if their relationships changed.

The issue, then, is not whether EP is a "bad" person for "putting pressure" on his family, or whether he's foolish in "risking" divorce, but whether *anyone* in his family system is healthy enough to operate on the basis of his own wants and needs, and whether EP is willing to maintain his position long enough to frustrate the others to the point where they will do the same. While it's possible a "breakup" may ensue, it's equally possible that everyone may end up living together and enjoying each other's company much more than ever before.

To examine relationships in your own family, you might want to check out things like:

(a) If you disagree with your family, do you do what you want anyway, or do you go along with them just to keep peace?

(b) If you go along with them, what "leverage" do they use to "make" you do it? (How do you scare yourself?)

(c) What would happen if they disagreed with you and you did what you wanted anyway? Would that be okay with you?

(d) Which (if any) of the people close to you, including your friends, are genuinely interested in your success? Which of them would not be comfortable with it?

(e) Do *any* of them *truly* share your desire for wealth and happiness?

(f) What would happen if you had no one to share your dreams and hopes for the future with? Would you give up, or go out and look for someone?

CHAPTER
THIRTEEN

Other People

EP: God! I never figured there was so much crap going on at the office.

M: How's that?

EP: Well, I decided to get clear about things, and what I saw was more than I had bargained for.

M: Like what?

EP: Well, we had a big staff meeting yesterday, like we do periodically, and boy, did I get an earful!

M: Oh!

EP: Yeah. The boss was away, and it was just pure chaos. (Pause) Wait a second. I've got some notes here about it. It was unbelievable. . . . Here they are. Let's see. . . . We all arrived at the meeting on time, but no one really knew what we were there for. We'd gotten an agenda, but it was pretty sketchy.

M: So?

EP: So everybody just sort of sat around waiting for something to happen. It got so bad that I finally decided to try and get some Natural Child energy and interest generated by asking everyone what they wanted to accomplish.

M: And?

EP: Did *that* go over like a lead balloon! Nobody answered. After a few seconds of silence somebody suggested we send out for some coffee. We all chipped in for it. Then someone said we ought to get back to the question of what we were meeting about, but *he* was in his Parent, which was the last thing I wanted. Nothing much happened for a minute or two, and then one of the women said she thought we'd better hurry up so we could get back to work.

M: You still didn't know what anyone wanted to accomplish?

EP: No, I didn't. So I started to bring the subject up again, when the guy across from me got into *his* Parent and said maybe I should shut up and listen.

M: Then what?

EP: Then somebody mumbled that I was supposed to know what the meeting was about before I showed up. *He* was locked into his Parent, too. I could see it on his face.

M: And then?

EP: Then all of a sudden I felt the need to defend myself rather than try to stay clear. It was like this guy had a strong urgency to keep things muddled, and I had to do something about it.

M: So?

EP: Well, what ran through my mind was that if I said *anything* to him, I'd be defending myself, and if I tried to defeat him, I might look like an agitator.

M: So what did you say?

EP: So I asked him why it was more important for him to tell me what I should do than to discuss what we wanted to accomplish. I wanted to get him out of his Parent, just like you do with me sometimes.

M: And what happened?

EP: Well, he just stared at me like I was crazy. Then somebody else told us both to stop arguing—which was even crazier still, because I wasn't trying to argue.

M: And?

EP: So I shut up for a while and everybody started talking about what they thought everybody else should do. They were *all* in their Parent! I was having a terrible time trying to keep things straight.

M: So?

EP: Well, I couldn't think straight with everybody talking from their Parent and their Adapted Child. The whole discussion centered around what people thought they *had* to do, what they were *afraid* to do, what they *didn't want* to do, and what they felt other people thought they *should* do. There were no Adult or Natural Child statements at all. The terrible thing is that these meetings have always been like this, but I never knew it before!

M: And what's the problem?

EP: My whole *week's* been that way! Whenever I ask people what they want to do, they never respond directly. They really don't *know!* In fact, the whole office is broken down into three camps. One bunch always parrots what the boss wants to hear, another never says anything one way or the other, and a third always gripes behind the boss's back but never does anything. No one seems to know why he's even there!

M: How is this a problem for you?

EP: Well, for the first time in my life I feel totally alone. There isn't a soul who sees what's going on besides *me!* And they're beginning not to like me. I think they see me as a troublemaker.

M: So?

EP: If I keep this up much longer, I'm not going to have any friends.

M: Keep *what* up?

EP: Trying to stay clear.

M: How do you mean?

EP: It's like I need some *support* to stay clear!

M: Support?

EP: Yes. It's hard enough to stay out of my Parent as it is, but when people are always urging me to get back *into* my Parent, or into my Adapted Child, I find it almost impossible to resist them.

M: So. It looks like you'll have to choose between clarity and friendship. (Pause) Are you willing to give up your friends?

EP: You mean it's that bad, huh?

M: Bad?

EP: Yes. You mean there's no in-between?

M: Not the way you've stated it. I've just heard you say the choice you need to make is between your friends and clarity.

EP: But why don't people want me to be clear?

M: People don't care if *you're* clear, they just don't want to be forced into seeing clearly themselves.

EP: But I'm not forcing them.

M: Oh?

EP: No! (Pause) How am I forcing them?

M: You tell me.

EP: Hmmm. (Pause) I don't know. I just don't want them forcing *me* into my Parent.

M: And how do you resist that?

EP: By trying to get them to stay clear.

M: Oh? Did you just hear yourself?

EP: Yes, I said I was trying to get them to stay clear.

M: *You* want *them* to stay clear! That's different from what they want for themselves.

EP: But *they* want *me* to stay confused, and that's different from what *I* want for *myself!*

M: It poses a problem, doesn't it?

EP: It sure does. I can't just quit my job!

M: Why not?

EP: Well, I need the money!

M: That poses another dilemma, doesn't it?

EP: (Very frustrated) *You're* no help!

M: What are you feeling right now?

EP: That I'm at a dead end.

M: What does that feel like?

EP: Hopeless.

M: How are you making yourself feel hopeless?

EP: Uh . . . I see myself not being happy where I am and not being able to leave.

M: You appear unwilling to see clearly enough to do anything about it.

EP: I do?

M: Yes. What would happen if you saw clearly enough to resolve all this?

EP: I'd probably leave my job and all my friends.

M: So?

EP: Well, I don't know why, but that's scary! I wouldn't have a job or any friends. Where would I be?

M: It sounds like having a job and having friends were important goals in the past.

EP: Isn't that normal?

M: Would you feel good if I said it was?

EP: Yes!

M: Would you feel *bad* if I said it wasn't?

EP: Yes. (Looking puzzled) Wait a minute. What are you doing? What's going on here?

M: I'm just demonstrating how much power you've given me. I can make you feel good or bad, just on the basis of what I say.

EP: Oh. Okay. I get it. (Pause) I did get carried away with wanting to be normal. But keeping my job, and my friends, *is* important to me.

M: Well, it looks like you've got another dilemma then.

EP: What do you mean?

M: People who become rich and happy may have jobs and friends along the way, but they're willing to see them as transitory.

EP: Transitory?

M: Yes. As they grow, and as they change the way they run their lives, most successful people exchange their old friends and their old jobs for new ones. Sometimes their friends grow and change *with* them, but if they do, it's because they've chosen to, and not because they *have* to or because someone else wants them to.

EP: Well, I don't see myself exchanging friends and jobs. I see myself just losing them.

M: What are you preventing yourself from seeing?

EP: What do you mean?

M: You just said you see only part of the process. How do you prevent yourself from seeing the rest of it?

EP: You mean the part where I get new friends and new jobs?

M: Right!

EP: Well, I just can't conceptualize it.

M: Do you *want* to conceptualize it?

EP: Yes! But I don't know how!

M: How do you think you *might*?

EP: Well, I'd have to fantasize about it.

M: Okay. Why not try it?

EP: (Thinking deeply) Well, the new friends I'd have wouldn't try to keep me in my Parent.

M: And?

EP: And since they wouldn't have any *need* to keep me in my Parent, they'd be operating in their Adult and Natural Child a lot.

M: And what about the type of job you'd have?

EP: Well, there'd obviously be a lot of freedom in it, because people wouldn't be Parenting me a lot.

M: Anything else?

EP: It would be interesting and exciting, so my Natural Child would get involved.

M: Okay. Now you have an idea of what sort of work to look for. How could you *find* this kind of job and these kinds of people?

EP: I'd have to *look* for them.

M: Will you?

EP: You mean as a special project?

M: I mean any way you want. So far, you've just decided that you *need* to look for them. That's different from actually deciding to *look* for them.

EP: Oh. I get it. (Pause) Yeah. I'll start looking for them. I might as well. I've got to do it sometime.

M: Good. Let me know how it turns out.

EP: Okay. See you later.

Comments

1. As you see more clearly, you automatically give up your old Parent and Adapted Child tapes. As you do this,

you'll often find that the Parent and Adapted Child responses of those around you no longer make sense to you. Things people say and do that you'd normally respond to may seem strange, irrelevant, or unnecessary. Efforts you make to elicit sensible responses from such people often meet with stares and frowns and other signs of confusion or distress. You may not be able to relate to many of these people in the same way you did before.

Although you'll always be able to find *new* ways to relate to those willing to share in the effort, others will simply continue to resist. (When they make a Parent statement, they'll expect a Parent response, and all your efforts to remain Adult or to turn on their Natural Child will simply not satisfy them.) Your choice will often be to return to your old ways in order to maintain your old relationships, or to give up these relationships (at least for the time being) if you prefer to maintain your new clarity.

Giving up your friends is not as heartless as it may sound. It's really a very natural process. As you get clearer, you'll seek relationships with people whose clarity and potential are closer to your own, and whose interest in using that clarity and potential fits with your own interest. You may still *care* for your old friends. You'll simply have less in common with them than you'll have with your new friends.

CHAPTER
FOURTEEN

Your Life Plan

EP: You know, Martian, I'm still wondering how all this will turn out.

M: How *what* will turn out?

EP: My life. I was thinking about it before, but we got off on another subject.

M: Well, how do you think it will turn out?

EP: I don't know.

M: All right, then. How would you *like* it to turn out?

EP: Why do you ask me that?

M: Because you already have in your mind an idea of how it will turn out.

EP: I do?

M: Yes. Most Earth People plan their lives when they're very young. You're no exception.

EP: I *planned* my life when I was young?

M: Yes.

EP: That's hard to believe. I can't think of any plan I ever made.

M: That's why I asked you to fantasize about it. You don't have your own permission to know your plan.

EP: You asked me to fantasize about it?

M: Yes. When I asked you how you'd *like* your life to turn out, I was essentially asking you to fantasize. Perhaps your

Natural Child will reveal some of the plan if you just let your mind roam over some of the possibilities.

EP: You mean if I fantasize about it, I might come up with something I wouldn't otherwise think to say?

M: Yes. Want to give it a try?

EP: Okay. (Pause) Let's see now. What I'd really like would be to live to be seventy-five or eighty, and to live a very full life. I'd like to have the freedom to do as I wish, to travel a lot, and to not have to worry about where my next paycheck is coming from.

M: How do you envision arranging for all this?

EP: Well, after I save up some money, I'm going to quit my job and take some time off to think about it.

M: Why wait until you quit your job?

EP: I'm too busy now.

M: So?

EP: I need time to sit back and relax before I can think about the future.

M: Why is that?

EP: I don't know. (Pause) It's just that it's too much of a burden right now to think about it.

M: Oh? Why is it a burden?

EP: That's hard to say. It just seems like it would be too much for me to do.

M: Too much?

EP: Yeah. I've got enough to think about already.

M: Enough?

EP: You're darn right! I have to think about myself, and my family, and keeping my job—at least until I find another. Sometimes just trying to survive is tough enough.

M: Are you expecting me to accept that?

EP: What do you mean?

M: It sounds as if you're trying to justify your inaction. As if you're trying to come up with an excuse that will satisfy someone else's Parent, just like you used to do when you were a youngster.

EP: But it *can* be too much for one person!

M: "Too much" and "enough" are Parent words. They're

judgmental. So is the notion that "trying to survive" is "tough." They sound like words meant to satisfy someone's Parent—particularly a Parent that has tapes in it about "struggling" and "hard work."

EP: Hmmm. You mean it's the sort of excuse I'd give to get my mother or father off my back?

M: Right. Now you're trying to get *me* off your back. You're trying to get me to accept the same excuse.

EP: You don't think it's reasonable, huh?

M: What *I* think isn't important. However, if your *own* Parent accepts it, you'll stop yourself from thinking any further about your life—until after you quit your job.

EP: What's wrong with that?

M: Nothing in itself. But it uses up time.

EP: Are you saying that I should hurry, instead? I just stopped doing *that,* you know!

M: I'm not saying you should hurry. I'm saying that you're stopping yourself from thinking about your future by waiting until you quit your job. If you keep stopping yourself, you may run out of time.

EP: Hmmm. (Thoughtfully) You may have something there. But I've already accomplished a lot. I've moved to smaller quarters to save money, you know. I went through all that hassle with my family, and got them to go along, and as soon as I've saved some money I'm going to start thinking about the future some more.

M: Okay. I notice that the word "after" seems to be important to you. You first said that you'd wait until "after" you'd saved some money. Then you just changed it to "as soon as" you've saved some money—possibly to make it sound more appealing, or to make the moment sound closer. But you're still not planning to do any thinking until *after* this event occurs.

EP: But what's the use of thinking about such things if there's nothing I can do about them? If I don't have the money to operate with, it's all just wishful thinking!

M: Do you hear your Parent in that statement?

EP: (Startled) What? Saying what?

M: Saying everything you just said. The whole statement about "what's the use," and the notion that thinking and fantasizing are "wishful thinking"!

EP: (Nodding slowly) Hmmm. That *is* judgmental, isn't it? (Pause) But it seems to make sense, somehow.

M: It's a good way to stop your Natural Child from fantasizing.

EP: What? By telling myself it's just wishful thinking?

M: Yes.

EP: (Pause) I think I see what you mean. People who succeed in life don't do that, do they?

M: No. They do just the opposite. They fantasize so much that they make their dreams come true.

EP: But how?

M: They learn about reality, and then they fantasize about how they could *change* that reality—to make it better, or prettier, or faster, or smoother, or more efficient, or anything else more valuable.

EP: How does this make their dreams come true?

M: *They* make their dreams come true by learning how to dream. Before starting to dream, they have a vision of something that's real—something they've seen, or read, or heard. Then they take in more reality data—information about how in practice their vision might be altered—and they pump it into their dream. What comes out is a dream that can come true—a picture of something that can actually be done, or in some way made to happen.

EP: But how do they get the reality data to pump into their dream?

M: They see it, or they hear it. It must not be something they've been shown, or told, by someone else's Parent. It must be information that is simply there, available to be seen or heard; and when they open their eyes and become available to see it, they simply see it.

EP: And how do they make their dream come true?

M: It's all in the dream. They learn how to do it in the dream.

EP: Is this a dream they have when they're sleeping, or can it be a daydream?

M: It's usually a dream they have when they're awake—at a time when they're enjoying life, in their Natural Child, and moving smoothly from reality to fantasy and back again.

EP: (Pause) Hmmm. So the plan I have for my life may not come true, because I don't know how to *make* it come true?

M: The *fantasy* you told me about how you'd like your life to turn out may not come true, because you don't know how to dream and make your dreams come true. But the *plan* you have for running your life will come true. It always does, for *all* Earth People, unless they die prematurely in an accident or natural disaster.

EP: Well, what is my *plan*? That's what I want to know!

M: Your plan may have several possible outcomes, depending upon which path you take.

EP: You mean I can alter the outcome of my life by the various decisions I make along the way?

M: Yes. If these decisions involve matters relating to the outcome of your life.

EP: Hmmm. I think I'm beginning to get a glimmer. Like, one path I might take would be to continue to wish for things but never get them, but another, if I learn to fantasize properly, would be to make my dreams come true—including my dreams about how my life will turn out.

M: Correct. So far, your life plan has either directed you, or permitted you, to reach this point in your life. You're starting to examine the plan itself, and if the plan didn't at least permit this examination, you wouldn't be doing it. Now the question is whether or not your plan will permit you to choose your own future.

EP: Hmmm. I always *have* had some nagging doubts about whether I'd ever get what I wanted. I guess that's why I've been so reluctant to talk about it.

M: Your doubts are well founded. You keep stopping

yourself. You take a step forward, and then you immediately stop. You decide to wait for a while, until *after*
something else happens.

EP: Boy! This is really subtle! If I can trick myself this
easily, how in the world will I ever be able to work things
out?

M: Just listen to your words. Watch what you do. Listen
and watch how you stop yourself.

EP: Hmmm. When in doubt, you always get back to
seeing and hearing, don't you?

M: Always.

EP: (Thinks)

M: Now, are you willing to give up your need to wait?

EP: I guess it really was just a last-ditch attempt to make a
struggle out of all this. But you caught me at it. It's amazing.
I don't think I could have caught myself. It all sounded so
reasonable.

M: I know. Almost all Earth People go through their lives
justifying the limitations they've placed on themselves.
That's how they keep their life plan intact.

EP: And stop themselves from getting what they
want . . .

M: Yes. But you know, you still haven't answered my
question.

EP: What? About giving up my need to wait?

M: Yes.

EP: Yeah. I *am* willing to give up my need to wait.

M: All right, then. Tell me how you're going to arrange
things so your life turns out the way you want it to.

EP: Well, I'll have to prepare some in-between steps. I
don't know any way it can all work out right now, unless I
make some provision for it to do so.

M: Good. What do you have in mind?

EP: I'm not sure, but I've been trying to activate my
Natural Child, and to think, or dream, creatively. Just as
we've been talking, I flashed on a picture of a piece of land I
saw yesterday—just an empty, vacant lot—and I envisioned
how someone might build a house on it that would enhance

the value of the property. Not a regular house, but a very special, attractive house. I also started thinking of a favorite pop tune of mine, and I thought about how they could have added an extra beat to the music, sort of an extra "catch" in the rhythm section to make it more appealing.

M: That's a fine start.

EP: I know it's a start, but my problem is that it's too late in my life for me to become an architect, and it would take too long to become a musician. So, being creative in these sorts of ways won't really help. I'm really stuck. I don't know what else to do!

M: How are you keeping yourself stuck?

EP: I really don't *know* how I'm keeping myself stuck!

M: Did you hear yourself say that it's "too late" to become an architect, and it would take "too long" to become a musician?

EP: Yes. I sure did!

M: What part of you said it?

EP: I don't know! Not for sure, anyway. It was probably either my Natural Child or my Adult. I certainly don't have the time to go through all the hassle and years of study to learn those professions. My Natural Child doesn't want to do it, and my Adult knows what a job it would be!

M: What part of you said you would have to do that—you'd *have to* go through all the hassle and years of study?

EP: Huh? What do you mean? How else could I make use of such ideas? I'd have to learn to expand them, formalize them, and put them down on paper! Do you know any other way?

M: There are many ways. What part of you said there was only one way?

EP: *Name* another way!!

M: What part of you is speaking right now?

EP: Don't bother about that! Just name some other ways to use ideas about building houses and writing music!

M: You seem to have a real urgency to stop thinking creatively.

EP: Huh? (Pause) What do you mean?

M: You stopped thinking creatively right after you started. And now you're much more interested in arguing with me.

EP: Hmmm. (Long pause) I *am* arguing, aren't I?

M: Yes. Do you know how you got into it?

EP: No. I don't.

M: Do you *want* to know?

EP: Yes! I certainly do!

M: Okay, then. Let's get back to where we were a moment ago. What part of you said that you *had to* go through a lot of hassle and years of study to make use of your ideas?

EP: Well, I thought it was my Adult, or my Natural Child, but now that you're stressing the "have to" aspect, I guess it was my Parent.

M: And why did you stop thinking creatively, just now?

EP: Because it's discouraging! I don't *want* to have to do all those things!

M: And which part of you said that you *had to*?

EP: My Parent.

M: Do you see how subtly your Parent entered your thought processes and cut off your creativity?

EP: (Pause) Oh, God! That's really awful! I hardly even got started, and my Parent cut right in!

M: That's right. And remember, you *learned* to operate that way. However, you can *re*learn it, and do it differently, if you want.

EP: (Incredulously) You're saying that I learned to cut in and stop myself whenever I had a creative idea?!!

M: Yes. All Parent behavior is learned. What happened when you were young was that whenever you had a creative idea, your mother or father would immediately cut in and evaluate it—usually in a negative way.

EP: How can you be sure of that?

M: *I'm* sure, because I'm a Martian. But *you* don't have to accept my word for it. If you watch your behavior, you can be certain that *something* like that happened, because there's no other way you could have learned to act like that.

EP: You mean that since it's part of my automatic behavior, I had to learn it somewhere? *Where* I learned it isn't as important as the fact that I'm presently doing it, and I can relearn it if I want to?

M: Right.

EP: Okay. I see what you mean. I'll keep my eye open for it in the future, and try to work on it when it comes up.

M: All right. (Pause) What are you thinking about right now?

EP: I'm thinking that I should look for some alternate ways of being creative, since the ones I came up with won't work. I have to find some different subjects to think about.

M: Do you hear your Parent saying you "should" look for alternate ways? And that you "have to" find some different subjects?

EP: Hmmm. Yes, I do.

M: If you stay in your Parent, will you find any?

EP: No. I won't. They have to come from my Natural Child. But what I want to know is, what direction should I look in?

M: Before I respond, let me ask you a question. How are you keeping yourself stuck?

EP: (Pause) By staying in my Parent.

M: Okay. That's important for you to know, and for you to remain aware of. There's nothing I can do unless you take responsibility for getting out of your own Parent.

EP: Oh. You mean that you could really say almost anything, and if I was still in my Parent it wouldn't do me any good?

M: Right.

EP: But I'm not sure how I get *into* my Parent! I don't know what it is that I should stop doing!

M: What was your Parent telling you when you got hung up about needing to become an architect or a musician?

EP: Hmmm. (Thinking) My Parent was pushing me. It was saying I better hurry up! Oh! Wow! (Pause) I thought I'd gotten over that! It was saying that I'd better hurry up, or I'd never work this all out!

M: Do you hear the urgency in it?

EP: Yes. And I know what you're going to suggest. If I take the urgency out—if I stop trying to push myself—I'll automatically get out of my Parent.

M: Good.

EP: But I still think I have a legitimate question. I've just found myself thinking creatively about a couple of subjects that won't do me much good. How do I find the subjects that *will* do me some good?

M: Do you hear yourself asking for a Parent response?

EP: (Looking startled) Well, I was trying to word my question carefully, but I did try, I guess, in sort of a round-about way, to get you to say "how" I should do something . . .

M: Yes.

EP: But I've asked you questions like that before, and you've answered me!

M: That's because there was no other way to talk to you. Your conversational patterns were very primitive. In fact, they still are.

EP: So why not continue? Why not just answer me?

M: It won't do you any good. You can't be told how to turn on your Natural Child. Your Natural Child turns *itself* on, when it knows it won't be interfered with by your Parent.

EP: Can't you even give me a hint about what direction to look in?

M: I've already done so. I've said to stay in your Natural Child. Your Natural Child will find a direction.

EP: But I've already been in my Natural Child, and it didn't work!

M: It didn't work because you got into your Parent, and stopped it from working.

EP: But I need help!

M: Is that how you got people to help you when you were young?

EP: What? By saying I needed help? (Pause) Of course it was!

M: No. By first getting stuck, and *then* saying you needed help.

EP: What do you mean? They're both the same thing!

M: No they're not. People usually won't help you unless they see that you're stuck. It's much more effective to get stuck first than to merely ask for help without being stuck!

EP: But why would I ask someone to help me if I weren't stuck?

M: That's exactly my point! It's easier to justify it when you appear to need help. (Pause) Why ask someone to help you at all?

EP: To get out of the dilemma, naturally!

M: You can get out of the dilemma by yourself.

EP: What are you saying? That I shouldn't talk to people?

M: No. I'm saying that if you use getting stuck as a justification for getting people to talk to you, you'll prevent yourself from thinking things through by yourself. You'll continue to *wait* to get rich. You'll wait until other people talk to you, or help you, instead of just going ahead and getting rich by yourself.

EP: You mean I've been using the need to talk to people as an excuse to justify waiting?

M: Exactly.

EP: Wow! That's heavy. How could you tell?

M: By watching you and seeing what happened. You became stuck, and told me you needed help. Then, by talking to me, you didn't get past your stuck point.

EP: You mean I didn't *have* to get stuck?

M: Getting stuck happens occasionally. What you didn't have to do was to ask for help. You could have backed up, or tried another direction, without asking someone else to suggest something.

EP: Hmmm. That's very interesting. If we connect this up to the life plan I'm supposed to have, it's as if part of my plan has been to wish for this freedom and money I've been talking about, and another part has been to make a real struggle out of it. I take one step forward, and then I wait. I make a stab in a new direction, and then I look around for someone to help me. I'm like a five-year-old!

M: And that's about how old you were when you started putting the plan together. Most of the things you're changing are things you've been doing the same way for a long time.

EP: Okay. But does this mean that I won't be able to talk to you anymore? If I have to stop looking for help from other people at my stuck points, does it mean that we can't have any more conversations?

M: No. You can *talk* to me. You just can't do it when you're stuck. You'll need to pass the stuck point by yourself.

EP: (Pause) Oh! *I* see what you mean! And all of a sudden I'm not stuck anymore! I remember that I was saying I'd thought about building a house on this piece of land, and improving the beat in a certain song I like, but that I couldn't do either because I couldn't become an architect or a musician, and that's when I stopped myself.

M: Right.

EP: And now I'm not stuck anymore! I just figured out what I could do. If I don't *stop* myself, I can just continue doing the same thing I was doing, but on a wide variety of subjects, and just for the fun of it! After a while I'll probably hit on something that really turns me on. Then I can concentrate on *it,* rather than continue to think randomly!

M: Fine. That's as good an approach as any. How did you get past your stuck point?

EP: I don't know. It was a cumulative effect. It was as if all the things I've been learning suddenly jelled. All of a sudden I just knew that my Parent had been stopping me, and that instant I was back in my Natural Child.

M: Congratulations!

Comments

1. When people first discover they have a life plan, they typically try to uncover their early decisions by delving into

their past and speculating about where they seem to be going in the future. They hope that by uncovering these decisions they'll be in a better position to decide whether or not they want to change them. While this approach seems logical, and sometimes helps people understand how they got the way they are, it seldom helps them uncover the decisions they need most to change, and it rarely helps them to *change* them.

Trying to uncover each and every decision you've ever made is like going on an archeological expedition; and even when you *do* find a decision, you usually won't know what to do with it. The only effective way to decide which decisions to change is by looking at what you're doing *in the present,* and by asking yourself, "What am I doing right now that I want to do differently?" In this way you not only find decisions to change, but you also actively change them, and *know* that you've changed them, simply by changing *what you do!*

Life is very much a continuum. What you've decided in the past has brought you to the present. And what you decide in the present *about your present actions* will take you to the future. By changing what you do *now* (and often changing a past decision in the process), you can redirect the future course of your life in any way you please!

Thus, whenever EP talks about changing his life plan, M's approach is not to discuss the plan, or the past, but to bring EP back to the present and examine how he's operating at that very moment! ("Do you hear yourself?" "What are you feeling?" "How does this serve you?")

2. Most of us experience life as victims—as if we have no control over what's happening to us. What usually escapes us is that we spend most of our time positioning ourselves—or setting ourselves up—so that things happen around us in ways that we intend.

In this chapter EP has a vision of how he'd *like* his life to turn out (living a full life, living to eighty, etc.), but another part of him (his Adult) knows that things may not turn out like that unless he does some changing. EP's life plan opens several paths to him, depending on how he positions himself in the near future. One path—the one he's currently traveling on—leads to an ending that isn't as pleasant as the one he'd *like* to have. The other, more desirable path requires EP to do some repositioning of himself before he can follow it.

This situation isn't unusual. Most of us have life plans that permit repositioning in midstream, if only we're willing to do it. The fascinating thing about this possibility is that the clearer you are about how you'd like your life to be, the greater the likelihood of your making it come true! This holds true not only for the long-term outcome of your life, but also for all your interim hopes and dreams along the way. The more "real" your dream is—the more complete, detailed, and vivid—the easier it will be to *make* it come true! (The more you learn to use your Natural Child, the greater your chances of increasing the "realness" of your dreams.)

3. A key aspect of many life plans has to do with our *timing* of events. (*When* they'll happen, and how we'll plan for them.) EP apparently makes such decisions on the basis of the concept "after." (He waits until *after* he moves to save some money. He waits until *after* he saves some money to think about his next move.) Others of us use notions like "until," "never," "always," "over and over," and "open-ended." ("I won't examine it *until* . . ." "I'll *never* examine it." "I'll *always* examine such things." "I'll examine them *over and over*, but I won't necessarily act on them." "I won't make any plans to examine them, but *I might examine them if* they happen to come up.")

Check yourself out to see which of these notions is your habitual response. Once you discover it, you'll also be able to uncover the many ways in which it limits your progress.

CHAPTER FIFTEEN

Dealing with Your Parent

EP: I wonder how all this is going to turn out.

M: How *what's* going to turn out?

EP: My life. I'm making some big changes, you know, and I'm wondering what's going to happen on down the road. Like, does it all turn out the way I want, or will I just go on struggling as I am now for the rest of my life?

M: Do you want to go on struggling?

EP: No. Of course not! Not if I don't *have* to!

M: You don't have to if you don't want to.

EP: What do you mean by that?

M: If you want to, you can stop struggling. You don't *have* to struggle. The struggle is only in your head.

EP: That sounds crazy. I'm obviously having a terrible time with all this. It's very difficult for me!

M: You don't have to struggle.

EP: (Pause) I guess I don't understand what you're talking about.

M: The part of you that's interested in struggling can stop struggling. You don't have to make it hard on yourself.

EP: Some *part* of me is struggling, when I really don't have to?

M: Yes.

EP: How can you tell?

M: By observing you. You're struggling. You even said so yourself.

EP: But what makes you say it's in my head? This struggle is *real*. I'm up to my neck in it!

M: What's real is that you're changing your life. What's in your head is that you're struggling.

EP: Why do you say it's in my head?

M: Your way of doing things reflects what's going on in your mind. I *see* you struggling, so I know your mind is saying your life is a struggle.

EP: But that's because it *is* a struggle!

M: No. It's merely a journey. How you travel on it is up to you. Your journey can be comfortable, if you want it to be. You can feel comfortable, or even eager and excited.

EP: Then why am I making such a struggle of it?

M: You have a *need* to struggle.

EP: That's amazing!

M: I know. The question now is, how long will you continue to have this need?

EP: Good grief, I don't know!

M: Will you need to struggle for the rest of your life?

EP: No!

M: Okay, then. How long do you think you'll need to struggle?

EP: Until it comes easy to me.

M: Until what comes easy?

EP: Making money and being happy.

M: It *could* come easy right now, if you didn't have this need to struggle.

EP: (Angry and frustrated) Damn! You said that before, and it disturbs me. You're implying that I'm making it hard for myself on purpose.

M: *Part* of you is.

EP: What part?

M: *You* tell *me*.

EP: Well, it wouldn't be my Natural Child or my Adult . . .

M: Okay.

EP: So that leaves just my Parent and my Adapted Child.

M: You're narrowing it down.

EP: (Pause) Well, my Parent says that *everything* about life is a struggle. That's the way I was brought up. Things just don't come easy.

M: What's "easy" for you?

EP: Well, something comes easy if I don't have to work for it.

M: If you don't *have to* work for it?

EP: Right.

M: Are you saying that something's easy when there's no "have to" attached to it—when your Parent isn't involved?

EP: Hmmm. (Pause) I guess I am. I never thought of it that way. (Thinking) And I'm also saying it's easy when there's no *work* involved.

M: And work is something you don't like to do—something you *have to* do but don't *like* to do?

EP: Yes.

M: Do you hear your Parent in that, too—the "have to"?

EP: Yes. I do. (Pause) I guess my Parent enters into things more often than I thought, and in very subtle ways.

M: That's right.

EP: Come to think of it, my Parent seems to get in on almost everything I do. Whenever I start doing something, it immediately starts interfering, telling me things I *have to* do to get what I want.

M: And then what?

EP: What do you mean?

M: What happens after your Parent starts telling you what you have to do?

EP: I start resisting! (Pause) That's what makes it so hard. I start *resisting!*

M: What part of you starts resisting?

EP: Well, it has to be my Adapted Child. (Face brightening) I must have been resisting my Parent, and the Parent in other people, all my life!

M: And what's been the outcome of this resistance?

EP: Life has been a struggle! Doing *anything* is a struggle! Even with this journey I'm taking—my Parent is saying that I have to do it in a certain way. Like, I have to take it one step at a time, or I have to follow a certain path.

M: You know, of course, that you can follow any path you want. All paths lead to the same place, so long as you choose them because you *want to* and not because you *have to*.

EP: Yes, I know.

M: How is it that your Parent gets in your way?

EP: I don't know. I've never thought about it. My Adult says that there are many ways to do things, but the *new* ways, the ones I haven't explored, are unknown to me. Since I don't know what they are, and often don't know where to *look* for them, it's scary. It's easier to turn back to my Parent for advice. Of all the possibilities, my Parent at least knows a few of them.

M: Do they work?

EP: I don't know. I hardly ever get to carry them out. It's usually such a struggle. (Pause) Actually, they do work, sometimes, but it takes so long to do them, and I struggle so hard, that I never get on to other things.

M: So the struggle takes up time. It delays your success.

EP: You bet! It takes up so much time that my whole *life* becomes a struggle!

M: (Pause) That's an important insight. Are you aware of it?

EP: What? That my life's a struggle?

M: No. That it's a struggle because of the conflict between your Parent and Adapted Child.

EP: Hmmm. (Pause) No. I hadn't been aware of it. That's interesting. I've never seen it in quite that light!

M: How long will you keep on struggling?

EP: Well, it seems to me that I've got two problems. The first is to turn off my Parent, and the second is to stop resisting my Parent when it comes on inadvertently.

M: You're almost right. But according to what you said before, your first problem isn't to turn your Parent off—at least not in this case—but to stop turning to your Parent for advice whenever you get scared.

EP: Hmmm. Yeah. You're right. (Pause) And my second problem is to stop resisting my Parent whenever it comes on—whether I've turned to it or not!

M: Right.

EP: That's really going to be a hard one. I don't want to just accept what my Parent says I should do. That's how I got into this mess in the first place. Lots of times my Parent just doesn't know what's best.

M: You don't have to *accept* what your Parent says just because you've stopped rejecting it or resisting it. You can assess what your Parent says, and *ignore* it, if you want.

EP: Gee! I never thought of that!

M: That's because you weren't permitted to ignore your parents as a youngster.

EP: It is?

M: Yes. If you'd been permitted to ignore them, you'd have had no need to resist. Resisting wouldn't have become so automatic.

EP: Wow! That's fascinating!

M: Yes, but it's also another issue. Let's get back to the one we're working on. (Pause) When will you give up your struggling?

EP: When I have the power to ignore my Parent, and when my Natural Child feels good enough so that I don't have to go to my Parent for advice.

M: What's stopping you from doing that right now?

EP: I don't have the power.

M: How are you keeping yourself from having the power?

EP: I'm diffusing my power. I'm using it for other things. I'm resisting my Parent, and at the same time my Parent is trying to force me to do what it says. I'm scaring myself, and I'm using the rest of my power just to try to stop feeling afraid.

M: When will you stop diffusing your power?

EP: I can't say for sure, but pretty soon now, I hope.

M: What has to happen first?

EP: I don't know. I guess I'll just have to feel confident enough to do it.

M: Confidence comes after you stop diffusing your power. Confidence is what Earth People feel when they *focus* their power. I'm wondering what has to happen *before* you become confident, *before* you focus your power. What has to happen to enable you to focus it?

EP: Hmmm. Well, I guess I have to have permission to focus my power.

M: Do you have your own permission?

EP: Not yet.

M: Why is that?

EP: Well, it's hard to say. Permissions come from my Parent, and my Parent certainly doesn't say that I should focus my power on becoming rich and happy. It says that I should focus on all these other things—like feeling guilty and working hard, hurrying and trying to please other people.

M: Even though your Parent doesn't tell you to focus your power on becoming rich and happy, does it say that it's *okay* for you to do so?

EP: I'm a little fuzzy on that right now. It's like it's *almost* okay, but not quite.

M: When will it be okay?

EP: When I really get my head together. When I stop confusing myself and am able to work everything out.

M: Why not before?

EP: Because I'd look silly.

M: How would you look silly?

EP: Struggling around, and not knowing how to go about it.

M: So?

EP: I'd look foolish, not knowing which way to turn!

M: You mean you have to know all the answers before you start out? You have to be perfect?

EP: Yeah. Sort of. I know it sounds silly, but I don't want to be the laughing stock of the neighborhood.

M: Which part of you will laugh at you?

EP: Huh?

M: You heard.

EP: You're saying that some part of me will be laughing at me?

M: Yes. It's not the neighborhood that will laugh at you. You will laugh at yourself. I want to know which part of you will do it.

EP: Hmmm. (Pause) Well, it must be my Parent, saying that I shouldn't make any mistakes, and then laughing at me whenever I do. Sometimes I'm so afraid of doing something wrong that I simply won't try it at all.

M: Go on. You're doing well.

EP: But I'm not really sure that all the laughter comes from my Parent. It's more like some older, nasty kids are making fun of me, and getting pleasure out of it. Would that be my Parent, or would it be my Adapted Child?

M: Your memory of the laughter, and of the situations in which you heard it, is in your Parent. The feeling associated with it is in your Adapted Child. Did your mother or father ever laugh at you?

EP: Not that I can remember. It was mainly the kids at school.

M: Can you remember any situations?

EP: Not precisely. It happened on so many different occasions. I sort of remember them all as a big jumble.

M: Can you hear the laughter, or picture it in your mind?

EP: Yes. But it doesn't sound like I'm laughing at myself. It sounds like the laughter's coming from somewhere outside me—from all these other kids.

M: That's to be expected. That's how your Parent developed. All the input originally came from outside you. Then you internalized it, and now it comes from inside you, even though it may still *seem* to come from outside, because you originally recorded it that way.

EP: Hmmm. So my memory of the kids laughing at me could be in my own Parent right now?

M: It *is* in your own Parent right now.

EP: (Pause) Oh! I'll bet I know how I do it! I have this mental image of kids laughing at me, and as I conjure it up before my eyes, I start feeling that old, scary feeling in my Adapted Child, that terrible feeling when people laugh at me; and then my Parent starts telling me not to do something foolish—not to do something the kids might laugh at me for. (Pause) That's really interesting! I *learned* all this, and I put it into my Parent myself! It's not something I got directly from my mother or father!

M: Right. In fact, you actually made a *decision* about it. Can you remember the decision?

EP: A decision? What kind of decision?

M: A decision about doing things people might laugh at you for.

EP: (Pause) Oh. I'd never risk it. I decided I'd never again risk having people laugh at me.

M: And are you aware of the process by which you force yourself to abide by that decision?

EP: Hmmm. Well, I guess it's this whole thing we've been talking about. I conjure up this picture of kids laughing at me, and then I get into my Parent–Adapted Child thing about it.

M: Right.

EP: It's as if all my decisions were recorded on tape and now they're reflected in whatever my Parent and Adapted Child get into.

M: Yes. That's an important insight. Once a decision gets down on tape, you don't have to think about it anymore. In fact, you *don't* think about it—the tapes replay automatically. A problem occurs only if you later want to *change* the decision because you now have two separate voices in your head telling you *not* to.

EP: Wow! That's fascinating! That's why most people stay locked into their decisions!

M: Yes. And they usually can see no way out. (Pause)

Okay. Now, are there any circumstances under which you *would* risk being laughed at?

EP: No. Absolutely not. I'd only try something if I knew I could do it absolutely perfectly.

M: What's this about being perfect?

EP: If I don't make any mistakes, there won't be anything to laugh at.

M: Did your parents care if you made mistakes?

EP: You bet they did. They hated mistakes. I had to do everything just right.

M: Did they punish you?

EP: You better believe it. I don't know which was worse—the fear of laughter, or the fear of punishment.

M: It sounds as if you've got both fears paired together in your head.

EP: I do?

M: Yes. Like, laughter is another form of punishment.

EP: Hmmm. I guess it is, in a sense. Actually, in many ways laughter is even worse than punishment. It's the worst *kind* of punishment.

M: And you could always avoid punishment by doing things perfectly?

EP: Yes. I certainly wouldn't be punished for being perfect. Usually, I'd even be praised!

M: And could you avoid being laughed at by doing things perfectly, also?

EP: Not always. Sometimes kids would just laugh at me to be cruel—simply because I was too small or something. But I always tried to avoid their laughter by doing as well as I could.

M: The same way you avoided other types of punishment?

EP: Yes.

M: When did kids laugh at you?

EP: Usually when I was trying to learn something.

M: What was funny about learning something?

EP: I stumbled around a lot. Some kids just thought the whole process of learning was funny to watch.

M: What did they think was funny?

EP: They were usually older than I was, and they already knew how to do most of the things I was learning.

M: So?

EP: I didn't *know* as much as they did!

M: But what was funny?

EP: *That's* what was funny. The fact that I didn't know as much as they did, and I couldn't do things as well.

M: Were you trying to be funny?

EP: No! I was dead serious!

M: Did you do things in a funny way? Was there something about the way you went about learning that encouraged them to laugh?

EP: Not that I know of. But it's hard to say. Maybe there was. I fumbled around a lot and asked a lot of dumb questions.

M: If you were in the same situation again, as a grown-up, would you be able to avoid the laughter problem?

EP: I sure would. I'd just hang around with younger people. The only reason the kids even had *time* to laugh at me was because they were older, and they'd already learned most of the things I was just getting to. If they'd been my own age, they'd have been too busy learning for themselves to find time to laugh at anyone else.

M: Good. Is there anything else you'd do?

EP: Yeah. I wouldn't ask dumb questions. I'd anticipate what other people were thinking, and explain the reasons behind what I was doing.

M: Okay. That sounds pretty clear. (Pause) Now that we've talked about it, do you understand why you weren't permitting yourself to learn how to get rich?

EP: Yeah. I wasn't permitting myself to learn *anything!* I've always been afraid of the laughter, or punishment, I was sure I was going to encounter if I risked trying to learn something new. And the reason I could be so sure of encountering it was that I was secretly planning to laugh at *myself*. It was all on tape in my own head.

M: Is it okay, now, for you to learn how to get rich?

EP: Yeah. I think it is. My Parent still isn't saying that I *should* get rich, but it's not standing in my way. It's not saying I *shouldn't!*

M: Okay. I heard you say that you *think* it's okay. You didn't say it *is* okay. Are you still uncertain?

EP: Well, I'm not *absolutely* certain. There may still be something standing in my way. But I won't be *laughing* at myself, and I won't be afraid to try things for fear I won't be perfect. But if there is something else, we'll have to deal with it later. I've had just about enough for now.

M: You've done plenty. You've taken a major step forward.

Comments

1. This chapter illustrates many ways in which our early decisions show up in normal conversation—particularly in the normal speech patterns of the Parent and Adapted Child. Many of these examples draw on material introduced in earlier chapters. Some are fairly well hidden, and you'll need to go back over the dialogue to be sure you've discovered them all! (Did you notice, for example, that EP has a "be perfect" Parent driver that is almost as strong as his "hurry up" driver?) Learning to spot these decisions in your everyday conversation is essential to developing your ability to see and hear clearly, so stick with it!

2. Most of us are brought up to believe there are certain "appropriate" ways to become successful (like being a doctor, lawyer, executive, technical expert, etc.), but unless our Natural Child goes along with our choice of career, we rarely achieve outstanding success in it. Even if we do succeed in some ways, it's often at the expense of being happy. Few of us learn to make a career of the things we really like to do, yet this ability is the single most important ingredient in becoming successful. A really successful person is one who can identify what his Natural Child wants, and then let his Adult figure out how to make it profitable!

3. Now that you've got an idea of how EP sometimes stops himself from doing what he wants in life, you might like to check yourself out. Here are some questions to give you a start:

(a) Do you avoid doing things because you're afraid of looking foolish, or because you're afraid people might laugh? (Who might have laughed at you when you were young? Who's going to laugh at you now?)

(b) Do you avoid doing things because you don't think you'll do them well? (What would happen to you if you failed?)

(c) Do you avoid doing things because you're afraid you'll be tricked, or trapped, in some way? (How do you convince *yourself* not to do them?)

(d) Do you have a need to "look good"? (Where did you learn "looking good" was important?)

(e) Do you have your own permission to do *anything you want*? (If not, how could you obtain it?)

(f) Do you look to others for approval before starting something? (What would happen if you went ahead without their approval?)

(g) Do you "give up" before you even start? (How did this serve you when you were young? Is it still a good plan, or have things changed?)

(h) Do you wait for someone to tell you how to proceed (or to give you suggestions) before starting? (Why not start on your own?)

CHAPTER
SIXTEEN

The Powerless Cycle

EP: Boy, do I feel miserable! I went to a party last night, and I ate and drank too much.

M: You've done this before, haven't you?

EP: Yeah. Sometimes I just can't help myself. I've got no willpower.

M: You really sound helpless.

EP: When it comes to overindulging, I am. At least at parties. But I'll get over it. I'll just take it easy today.

M: Do you like the feeling?

EP: What feeling?

M: The feeling of helplessness. The feeling you described as having no willpower.

EP: (Pause) I don't really mind it. It's the morning after I don't like.

M: You really *like* not having any willpower?

EP: Well, when you put it that way, no. But it usually doesn't last for long.

M: Of course not. You get rid of it by stuffing your mouth with food and drink, and feeling bad the next morning!

EP: Yeah. I guess I do. But it goes away. It doesn't bother me much.

M: Then why do you look so bad?

EP: (Pause) What do you mean? Do I really look that bad?

M: You look terrible.

EP: Well, maybe I did overdo it a bit.

M: You overdid it a *lot!*

EP: Yeah. I guess so.

M: You seem to punish yourself like this quite often.

EP: Punish myself?

M: You certainly don't look *comfortable*.

EP: Oh.

M: How long has this been going on?

EP: What? Eating and drinking more than I should?

M: Yes.

EP: Well, I've always eaten a lot. I've kind of had a weight problem since I was a kid. Drinking came later. But I don't see what's so important about it.

M: These excesses occur when you feel powerless. They're symptoms of unfinished business in your life.

EP: Unfinished business?

M: Yes. Things from your early life that you haven't resolved. Things that still bother you.

EP: But what's this got to do with becoming rich and happy?

M: So long as you're still carrying around unfinished business, you can't get on with changing the rest of your life. You'll lack the power you need to gain control over your behavior.

EP: You mean unfinished business keeps me from having power?

M: Yes. Actually, your unfinished business involves all those situations where you were forced into powerless positions against your will when you were young. What's unfinished is that you need to take back your power.

EP: But what's this got to do with eating?

M: When you were in these powerless situations— situations you really couldn't get out of—you frequently tried to avoid the *feeling* of powerlessness by turning to something you actually had power over. For you, it was eating. You could always put things into your mouth, even if you couldn't control other aspects of your life. By eating, you could start feeling powerful again.

EP: You're saying that my eating was an effort to feel powerful when I was really feeling powerless?

M: Yes. But it never really worked. You never stopped feeling powerless for any length of time. What happened was that you programmed yourself to both feel powerless, and then eat in an attempt to feel powerful. Later, you'd feel powerless all over again. You recorded the whole sequence, rather than just getting rid of the powerless feeling.

EP: Wow! That's really amazing! (Pause) But how does it connect up to my overeating yesterday? I know that I didn't have any willpower—that I couldn't stop myself from eating, once I got started. But what else was going on?

M: Not having any willpower is another way of saying you felt helpless, or powerless.

EP: Okay. I'll buy that, but I started feeling powerless *after* I began eating, not before. It was my *eating* that I didn't have the willpower to stop.

M: Not quite. You may not have been *aware* you were feeling powerless until after you began eating, but if you check back, you'll find you were feeling powerless before eating, too. If you hadn't been, your urgency to eat wouldn't have been so strong.

EP: Hmmm. You've got a point there. I really did go for the food sort of automatically. (Pause) But I still don't understand all this.

M: Do you want to stop feeling powerless?

EP: Yes, I do.

M: Okay, then. Let's focus on your eating habits for a while. What do you feel when you're about to really stuff yourself?

EP: Feel? I feel *hungry!*

M: What kind of hungry?

EP: What do you mean?

M: What are you hungry for? Food? Affection? A certain *kind* of food? Rest? Relaxation? Sleep? Sex?

EP: (Pause) Usually I'm hungry for sweets! Candy, cake, or pie!

M: Is it the same kind of feeling you get when you sit down for a quiet steak dinner?

EP: Oh, no! It's more like a drive that I can't control. When I gorge myself on sweets, or even when I drink a six-pack of beer, I'm pretty much out of control. I barely taste what I'm swallowing!

M: Oh?

EP: Yeah. It involves a different kind of hunger from when I just need a regular meal. It isn't a physical, stomach hunger.

M: Can you be more precise?

EP: Hmmm. (Pause) I get real nervous, and anxious. Yeah. And sometimes I get angry. It's like I'm attacking the food when I wolf it down. I feel really good when I'm in the process of eating it, and then right afterward I feel guilty and kind of empty. Almost sad inside. (Pause) Gee. I've never thought of it like this before. It sure does seem like a lot's going on. It all just kind of snapped into focus when you asked me about being hungry for a steak dinner.

M: Do you notice any feeling *before* your first hunger pangs?

EP: (Thinking deeply) Yes. Yes I do! Sometimes I feel lonely or bored—or mildly depressed. And sometimes I feel downright blah. Almost . . . empty.

M: As if you need filling up or energizing?

EP: Oh, yes. Exactly! That's why I *eat!* It's as if the energizing I need, or the filling up, can be accomplished by filling up my stomach.

M: And can it?

EP: Well, somewhat. But it never lasts, and I inevitably get fat. I'm very energized when I'm attacking my food —especially if I'm really feeling anxious or angry. Sometimes it may last for a while, but afterward I feel sort of guilty and empty again, even though my stomach may be full. (Thoughtfully) You know, this eating thing seems to have a regular cycle, with a beginning, middle, and end. I feel certain things *before* I eat, certain things *while* I'm eating, and certain things *after* I eat.

M: Exactly. And this cycle is your method of dealing with your feelings of powerlessness.

EP: The powerless feelings start right at the beginning, huh?

M: Yes.

EP: So you're saying that boredom, and loneliness, and depression, and even feeling empty are all various forms of feeling powerless?

M: Of course. Just examine them. When you're bored, what is it you feel powerless to obtain?

EP: (Thinking deeply) Something to interest me! I can't find something to interest me, or something that might be exciting!

M: And when you're lonely?

EP: (Thinking some more) Well . . . companionship. Or someone to talk to. When I'm lonely I have no way of finding someone to talk to.

M: And when you're depressed?

EP: That's a tricky one. (Pause) It's sort of like I just can't get any *fun* out of life!

M: All right. Now how about when you feel empty?

EP: When I feel empty, I feel that I can't get *back* something that's been taken away from me. It's almost like my insides have been ripped out and taken away!

M: Can you hear the powerlessness in all these feelings?

EP: Yes. And the anger—particularly the anger in feeling empty. (Pause) But how do I deal with all this? How do I stop feeling powerlessness?

M: Allow yourself to experience all the feelings. Use them as a signal that you're in a powerless cycle.

EP: But what if I *don't* experience them?

M: Are you afraid to experience them?

EP: Oh, God! You should only know! If I were to really get in touch with my anxiety, I think I'd go crazy!

M: Oh? What does "go crazy" mean to you?

EP: I'd lose control of myself, and maybe jump out of a window or something.

M: Anything else?

EP: Or hurt somebody . . . maybe even *kill* somebody!

M: That doesn't sound like anxiety. It sounds like anger.

EP: (Pause) Hmmm. It sure does. But if I'm really angry, why does it feel like anxiety?

M: Because it's safer to feel anxiety.

EP: Safer? (Pause) Safer than what?

M: Safer than feeling angry.

EP: Hmmm. (Thinking) Why is that?

M: When you were young, did you feel angry very often?

EP: Sure. But I got scolded a lot whenever I had a temper tantrum.

M: What did you learn from that experience?

EP: That anger was something to avoid. Everybody else got upset when I got angry! I'd get punished pretty bad. I learned to avoid feeling angry at all costs!

M: And what did you begin to feel, whenever an anger-producing situation approached?

EP: Well . . . anxious, I guess. I began to feel anxious.

M: And what happened when you felt anxious, but *not* angry?

EP: (Thinking) What do you mean?

M: What happened in the family?

EP: Nothing. No one noticed. (Pause) Hmmm. (Looking surprised) I see what you mean! I guess it *was* safer to feel anxious!

M: Okay, now. What do you think you decided about feeling angry, in general?

EP: I decided not to feel it . . . I decided to feel anxious, instead.

M: Very good. You're making great strides. (Pause) Now, are you still afraid of feeling angry?

EP: Yes, I am. I think I might do something dangerous. Something really bad.

M: Like what?

EP: Well, as I said before, maybe kill somebody. Wouldn't anger bother *you* if you thought you might kill someone?

M: There's a difference between *feeling* violent feelings and *doing* violent things.

EP: You don't think I'd do something awful?

M: You don't *have* to. There's no need to connect what you feel with what you do. There are many healthy ways to express your anger.

EP: Then why am I so hung up on it? Why do *I* think I might kill someone?

M: To justify your decision to avoid feeling angry. It *sounds* reasonable to many Earth People, but it's merely your Parent justifying your early decision to avoid anger.

EP: Oh, wow! (Looking surprised) You're saying that it's all in my Parent?

M: Yes. There isn't any automatic connection between what you feel and what you do. You *learned* there was when you were a youngster, but it's really not so.

EP: Gee. That's funny, because when I think about it, I'm not even sure what I'm angry about! (Pause) I'll bet it has something to do with that unfinished business you were talking about, doesn't it?

M: Yes, it does. Can you recall any mealtime experiences that relate to anger?

EP: Let's see. I can hear my mother insisting on my finishing everything on my plate. She always piled on more food than I could possibly eat, and then she'd tell me how lucky I was compared to the starving children in China, or some such place.

M: How did you feel then?

EP: Angry. Damned angry! She made me eat until I was uncomfortable, and if I complained, I got yelled at!

M: Oh?

EP: Yeah. It was like I wasn't even in charge of my own body. There I was, nailed to the chair, being constantly forced to eat things against my will!!

M: You felt sort of powerless, like there was no way you could win?

EP: Why, yes. Exactly.

M: So! Now we know what you've been angry about! That must have felt terrible!

EP: (Eyes opening wide) Oh, God! That's really something! And since complaining was never an option for me—since I had no way to vent my anger—what I ended up doing was shoveling down my food and suffering in silence!

M: You shoveled down food?

EP: Yeah. And I really felt good about it. I got *even,* and I felt really victorious!

M: But I thought that was what you were *resisting!* I thought you didn't *want* to eat!

EP: Yeah. You're right. (Looking puzzled) That doesn't make sense, does it?

M: (Pause) Well, it makes sense if you look at it as your final attempt to feel powerful in a powerless situation.

EP: Eating? And then feeling victorious?

M: Yes. How did you get even and feel victorious?

EP: By eating . . . somehow. It was sort of an "I'll show *you*" revenge type of eating.

M: But it was more than just eating. What else was involved?

EP: Well, I was eating, and I didn't even look angry!

M: But you *were* angry?

EP: I was *livid!!*

M: Then how did you become victorious?

EP: Oh! I know! I *tricked* her! I tricked my mother. She thought that I'd given in—that she'd won. She saw me eating and didn't see my anger. That way I had the last laugh. I literally stuffed my mouth, and she thought I was enjoying it!

M: (Speaking emphatically) And that, right there, is the heart of your unfinished business.

EP: (Pausing as if startled) Huh? What is?

M: Tricking people.

EP: (Pause) In what way?

M: You don't have to trick people anymore, and you don't have to trick yourself.

EP: Trick myself? What do you mean?

M: You know.

EP: (Laughing sarcastically) Hah! Hah! You mean I trick myself when I eat?

M: Did you hear yourself laugh?

EP: When? Just now?

M: Yes.

EP: Sure! I thought it was pretty funny!

M: What part of you was laughing?

EP: (Pause) I guess it was my Child—my Natural Child.

M: Tricking yourself isn't natural. It's against your own best interests. Your Natural Child wouldn't laugh at that. Your Natural Child would feel angry.

EP: Oh. Then I guess it was my Adapted Child. Yeah. It really was my Adapted Child. It's an old tape.

M: What was your Adapted Child laughing at?

EP: That I was putting something over on my mother!

M: But your mother hasn't been making you eat for a long time now. The only part of her that's left is in your own Parent. You've been putting something over on yourself all these years, and laughing at yourself as you did it.

EP: (Pause) God! That's really sick!

M: Many Earth People do it. In fact, almost everyone who's overweight has some similar problem.

EP: Okay. But how do I do it? How do I actually trick myself?

M: You become aware of feeling powerless at some level—you feel lonely, or bored, or depressed—and when you start trying to do something about it, something that would make you feel *powerful,* your Parent intervenes. It says you *shouldn't* feel powerful. Sometimes it intervenes even before you *start* trying to do something. So you're caught in a bind, the same bind you were in as a youngster. And you find the same solution. You trick yourself into feeling some temporary power, a *little* power, by eating and feeling victorious—although you rarely recognize it as feeling victorious at the time. You just think of it as feeling "better."

EP: It sounds so simple when you put it that way.

M: It can be simple once you see the sequence. But we haven't finished looking at the whole sequence yet. Do you have any idea why you feel guilty, and then sad, after you've finished eating?

EP: Yes! After all you've told me the rest is easy! I usually feel guilty because I believe that I shouldn't try to be powerful—which is what I've just done, in my own powerless way. And then I feel sad because it's a pretty terrible bind to be in. It *is* sad!

M: And your final sadness returns you to your programmed status of feeling powerless. The cycle ends, and then begins again.

EP: (Dumbfounded)

M: Do you see it all?

EP: (Still stunned) I think so, but let me review it for a moment. I want to get a handle on the whole thing. First, I feel powerless in some way; bored or something. Then I feel angry. (Pause) But wait a minute! Why do I feel angry?

M: Anger's a natural reaction to feeling powerless. It's the start of returning to feeling powerful.

EP: Oh. Okay. But since my Parent doesn't allow me to feel angry—which I guess is a form of power—I switch my anger to anxiety. Then, somehow, hunger enters into it, because I connect the "filling up" that I need emotionally in a powerless position with the "filling up" I can get physically by eating. (Pause) But that doesn't really make sense. Hunger isn't an emotional Adapted Child feeling like the rest of these feelings. Why did I include it in the sequence?

M: It was natural for you to do so, because many of your power struggles occurred at mealtime. It may not make sense logically, but it makes sense to a youngster who's grasping at any straw he can find to make himself feel better.

EP: Hmmm. (Thinking) It's the one nonlogical connection I made, which created the symptom of being overweight and eating too much.

M: Right.

EP: Okay, now. Let's see if I can get the rest of this straight. As I eat, my hunger disappears, and turns into a form of temporary power that makes me feel victorious. This is actually the main feeling I *trick* myself into feeling, because my Parent says I shouldn't feel powerful. But it doesn't last long. I immediately revert to feeling guilty and sad, because my Parent has bought into the whole thing all along and I don't see any way out of it.

M: Superb.

EP: So the whole sequence of feelings goes like this: I feel powerless, then angry, then anxious, then hungry, then victorious, then guilty, and then sad.

M: That's it.

EP: But now that I understand it all, what do I *do* about it? How do I stop the cycle?

M: Turn off the tape that says you shouldn't feel powerful. Give yourself permission to feel powerful.

EP: (Pause) But you don't understand! When I was young that was the most sensible tape I put into my Parent! You don't know how terrible things were when I got angry!!

M: Those situations don't exist now. The only times you feel powerless now are when you create the feelings or situations for yourself.

EP: I hear you saying that, and I know it must be true, but I still feel myself resisting.

M: That's one of your options. You can keep following the whole cycle if you like, but it's an enormous drain of energy. You can choose to use your energy to feel happy and get rich, or you can choose to use your energy to engage in power struggles from your past.

EP: (Thinking) Hmmm. That's really what this is, isn't it? It's really a power struggle from my past. A struggle with my mother over food.

M: Over *power,* not food! Meals merely provided the arena.

EP: (Pause) Okay. I buy all we've said about feeling powerless when I really wolf down my food, but what about all the other times when I'm really feeling pretty powerful but I *still* stuff my face? There are plenty of times when I overeat and I don't feel *powerless!*

M: These are situations where you're preventing yourself from *maximizing* your power. You're telling yourself you shouldn't feel *really* powerful; just moderately powerful. It's still a power struggle. It just differs in degree.

EP: You don't leave me much choice, do you?

M: The choice is yours. You can choose to feel very powerful, moderately powerful, or not at all powerful. If you want to get rich, you must feel very powerful.

EP: Hmmm. And you think I can do it, huh?

M: Sure! If you haven't maximized your power, it's because you're using your energy inside yourself in an internal power struggle, rather than outside yourself, focused on some external goals. You already *have* the power. The decision is how you choose to use it.

EP: Well, the reason this finally makes sense to me is that I can *feel* the way I tie up my energy inside myself. It seems to me that if I just stop doing that, I ought to have lots of energy left over.

M: Good. Now that you're getting a sense of what you feel, you're already beginning to increase your power. Soon, if you keep at it, you'll be able to have anything you want!!

Comments

1. The issue in this chapter is, of course, not that you have to be thin in order to become rich and happy, but that you need to regain your personal power. The most meaningful examples of how to regain your power involve those situations where you've most clearly lost it. Some of the best illustrations involve compulsive behavior—those moments when we lose our "willpower," when one feeling of powerlessness blends into another, and then another, until we seem totally unable to gain control over what we're doing.

Although many people don't see their constant battle with weight in those terms, eating is one of the most common examples of compulsive powerlessness in our society (closely followed by smoking cigarettes and drinking alcohol). More childhood power struggles occur at the dining table than at any other single place. The issue of consuming food provides a classic example of how someone can lose his power, and demonstrates the sort of decisions he needs to make in order to regain it.

The best way to learn to regain your personal power is simply to give up your compulsive behavior, whatever it may be. (Can you envision feeling comfortable and satisfied when eating, or drinking, or spending money if you never have in the past? Can you imagine the energy you'd release, and be able to use for other things?) The best place to start is with some small compulsion, and then build up to the bigger ones.

2. All our feelings of powerlessness are based on early experiences when our power was somehow taken away from us—or when we, for some reason, decided to give it up. These moments usually occurred when we weren't permitted to express ourselves openly, or show we were feeling a Natural Child feeling of power (usually anger, frustration, or sexuality). Our decision to substitute more acceptable behavior often involved substituting more "acceptable" (and less powerful) feelings. These decisions were almost always detrimental to us. We hardly ever agreed fully with the action we took, nor enjoyed the feelings we substituted.

Unable to express our real feelings, we soon convinced ourselves that the powerless, Adapted Child feelings we substituted were our real feelings. They became familiar, and, in a sense, comfortable. We learned to perpetuate them by stringing them together, one after the other, in various sequences. (Since we weren't permitted our real feelings, we really had little choice.) In some cases this process actually became circular, interrupted only by a brief moment of victory or vengeance (which was the closest we could come to the real feeling of power we weren't permitted to have).

Deciding to feel powerful, and breaking this cycle, is one of the most useful exercises you can undertake! You may not have to recall your early experiences in as great detail as EP, and you may not have to be able to identify the sequence of your feelings with such precision. But you *will* need to recognize your powerless situations, and decide to take your power back! Permit yourself to feel powerful! *Redecide* your earlier decision!

CHAPTER
SEVENTEEN

EP Stops
Tricking Himself

M: How are you doing with your eating habits?

EP: "Skinny City" here I come! I really seem to be making headway! While I've only lost a few pounds so far, I feel my eating habits are more under control.

M: That's good to hear. Do you notice any other changes in your behavior?

EP: You mean, like feeling powerful?

M: Yes.

EP: Well, I really *do* feel more powerful, just because I'm not worrying so much about food. I smoke a bit more than I used to, but that's better than eating too much.

M: Another way to trick yourself, eh?

EP: What?

M: Smoking involves the same sort of power struggle as eating. It's another way to trick yourself into thinking you're feeling powerful. But the feeling never lasts.

EP: Smoking is a power struggle like eating?

M: Absolutely.

EP: But I really worried about my eating. Smoking makes me feel relaxed, and I don't feel bad afterward.

M: I see. (Pause) What would happen if you quit smoking?

EP: (Thinking) Well, to be truthful, I'd probably be a nervous wreck!

M: Anxious?

EP: Well . . . yes.

M: So you smoke in order to stop feeling anxious?

EP: You could put it that way. But it's *more* than that. I actually feel *better* after smoking. I feel physically relaxed.

M: What you feel afterward is a separate issue from why you start.

EP: It is?

M: Yes. How old were you when you first started smoking?

EP: About fourteen.

M: And what did your parents think about it?

EP: They both smoked a lot, but they didn't want *me* to.

M: What did they say about your smoking?

EP: They didn't know that I smoked because I used to sneak into the bathroom and open all the windows.

M: How did that feel?

EP: Actually, it was kind of exciting. They didn't find out about it until years later. All us kids used to do it.

M: What would have happened if your parents found out?

EP: I would have caught holy hell. They didn't like disobedience.

M: So you really tricked them pretty well then, didn't you?

EP: I sure did!

M: How did you feel when you tricked them?

EP: As if I'd really *won* something! I showed them they couldn't stop me from smoking!

M: A real victory, eh?

EP: Yup.

M: Now do you see the relationship to your eating?

EP: Hmmm. You mean feeling victorious?

M: Yes.

EP: (Pause) Well . . . somewhat.

M: Okay. What did you feel next, after feeling victorious?

EP: I'd air out the room and flush the butts down the john, and then I'd relax! I'd feel quite satisfied with myself.

M: Victorious and satisfied?

EP: Kind of. Although I'd wish I didn't feel as if my folks were looking over my shoulder.

M: So you didn't feel totally satisfied?

EP: No. I guess I didn't. Are you suggesting that I was really feeling powerless?

M: No, I'm not. Where in the sequence would *you* say you felt powerless?

EP: (Thinking) Hmmm. (Pause) Well, if I had to pick a point, it would be right at the beginning when I was told I couldn't smoke, and I wanted to. That's a pretty powerless position to be in.

M: Okay. And what did you feel right *after* you were told you couldn't smoke?

EP: Angry! But I didn't *say* anything. I kept it to myself.

M: And what did you feel right before you decided to sneak into the bathroom?

EP: Angry, still! I was pretty teed off that my parents smoked themselves, and still had the nerve to tell me not to!

M: You didn't feel powerless for long, did you?

EP: No, sir! (Pause) That's the same pattern as eating, isn't it? I felt powerless, and immediately after, I felt angry!

M: Yes. And what did you feel next?

EP: I don't know. As I visualize myself there in the bathroom . . . I guess the next thing I felt was excitement.

M: What kind of excitement?

EP: Like you feel when you're doing something you know you shouldn't. Like, when you're afraid you might be caught.

M: Did this have anything to do with feeling that your folks were looking over your shoulder?

EP: Yes. In a way. I was a little anxious about that. (Pause) I guess I was feeling anxious and excited at the same time

M: And how did you get rid of the anxious feeling?

EP: By smoking! When I really got into smoking, I started feeling victorious—like I was putting something over on my folks.

M: Oh? Did you just hear yourself?

EP: Yes. (Pause) That's interesting. I said that I stopped myself from feeling anxious by smoking. But . . . I don't quite know how to say this . . . it was a different kind of anxiousness than I feel nowadays before I start to smoke.

M: I know. But let's just deal with the anxiousness you felt *then,* and get the sequence straight.

EP: Okay.

M: It looks like you felt powerless, then angry, then anxious, and then you smoked. Then you felt victorious, and then relaxed and satisfied. The smoking came right between feeling anxious and feeling victorious.

EP: That *is* just like my eating, isn't it? My eating also came right between feeling anxious and feeling victorious!

M: Yes. And since this is a powerless cycle, it probably didn't end with your feeling satisfied. You felt something *later* that returned you to feeling powerless again.

EP: Guilty. (Pause) I felt guilty. I don't want to make this all sound too pat, but the truth is that I eventually felt guilty about it all.

M: Okay. Now you understand the whole cycle.

EP: (Pause) And you think that my feeling victorious in the middle of this cycle was an effort to regain the feeling of power that I'd lost at the beginning?

M: Absolutely. But you must understand that you lost your power here in a different way than when you were eating. There, your power was taken away from you by your mother. Here, you gave it up all by yourself.

EP: I *gave* it up?

M: Yes. You decided that you wanted something that you couldn't have—your parents' permission to smoke. You didn't *have* to decide that. By doing so, you induced your own feeling of powerlessness.

EP: I didn't want their permission! I just wanted to smoke!

M: No. You wanted their permission.

EP: How do you know?

M: If you hadn't wanted their permission, you wouldn't have felt powerless, and you wouldn't have *needed* to feel victorious.

EP: I don't understand.

M: Their permission was the one thing you were powerless to obtain. You weren't powerless to smoke. You did smoke, so you obviously had the power to do so. What you didn't have the power to do was smoke with your parents' permission, because *they* had the power to withhold that permission. By wanting something you couldn't have —something someone else could deny you—you made yourself feel powerless.

EP: Oh! (Pause) You mean *any* time I want something someone else won't give me, I'll automatically feel powerless, because in reality *they* control what I want?

M: Right. And you'll *continue* to feel powerless as long as you continue wanting it.

EP: But in this case I didn't continue to feel powerless. I switched to feeling angry and victorious!

M: They were both part of the powerless cycle you kept yourself in.

EP: Hmmm. That's very interesting. (Pause) Actually, I could have avoided the whole problem by just deciding I didn't want to smoke in the first place.

M: No. That would have been even more harmful. Your problem was that you felt powerless. The only way you could avoid it was to decide you didn't want *permission* to smoke. Deciding you didn't want to smoke at all would have been something quite different.

EP: Why do you keep emphasizing that?

M: Because deciding not to smoke at all is a broader decision than deciding not to want permission. If you make a broader decision than you need to make in order to regain your power, you'll *lose* more power than you'll gain.

EP: Why is *that*?

M: The basic source of human power is to *want!* To want

something impossible is a drain of power, but to decide not to want something that *is* possible, without examining it separately, is cutting off your power at its source.

EP: (Eyes lighting up) Oh! *I* get it! You're saying that if I used this situation—where all I wanted was my parents' permission—to stop myself from wanting something *more* than just their permission—from wanting to smoke, for example—then I'd be needlessly cutting off my power before I'd fully explored the possibilities!

M: Right!

EP: Wow! (Pause) The trick is to know what's really obtainable! If it's not obtainable, I'm losing power by bothering with it. If it *is* obtainable, I'm losing power by excluding it.

M: Yes. The trick is to actually keep your power in places where you have it, and not give it away in places where you don't.

EP: Huh?

M: You just think about it for a while. Your statement wasn't wrong. It *is* important to know what's obtainable. But it's even more important to focus on your power.

EP: (Thinking) Oh. Okay.

M: Now, if you've been following this closely, there's something else you can learn. You'll see that your power struggle over eating occurred when your mother wanted something of you which *you* resisted. The struggle over smoking, however, occurred when you wanted something of your parents which *they* resisted.

EP: Hmmm. (Pause) That's really interesting. I never thought of it that way. It's like you can want something actively, and feel powerless, or you can merely resist, and feel powerless also. (Pause) Hmmm. Can it be that both sides in a power struggle feel powerless?

M: Yes. The *active* person can feel powerless, too. That's why when you weren't eating, your mother had to resort to forcing food down your throat or tricking you into eating it. She needed to regain the feeling of power she lost during your resistance.

EP: (Looking startled) God! To think that things like that go on between mothers and children!

M: It happens all the time.

EP: And how did my parents regain their feeling of power in the struggle over smoking?

M: They didn't have to. You gave it back to them by tricking them into thinking you weren't smoking.

EP: Oh! Wow! You mean they automatically felt powerful again because they thought they'd won?

M: Right.

EP: Gee. That's really amazing. (Pause) You know, it's funny. Life is really a series of incidents where you feel powerful, lose the feeling, and try to get it back again—usually at the expense of the people around you.

M: That's pretty accurate.

EP: And these basic power struggles seem to be the source of most of the Adapted Child feelings that interfere with our lives. Rather than feel powerless, we feel all these other feelings instead, and keep ourselves tied up in knots.

M: That's right.

EP: Is this why, back when we first met, you said it was so important for me to know what I feel—so that I could know when I was feeling powerless?

M: Absolutely.

EP: So that once I recognized it, I could stop the feeling?

M: Yes.

EP: And how *can* I stop feeling it?

M: You tell me. We've already talked about it.

EP: (Pause) Oh. I know. I can turn off the Parent tape that says I should feel powerless.

M: Right.

EP: Okay. I'm with you. But what about my anxiousness? Is it always a coverup for feeling powerless?

M: Sure. You felt anxious when you sneaked into the bathroom to smoke, because you knew that you were ultimately powerless to stop your folks from finding out—if they really wanted to. They could always interrupt you in the bathroom, smell the smoke, or check your clothes for cigarettes if they suspected something.

EP: But the type of anxiousness I feel nowadays before smoking has nothing to do with fear of being caught!

M: No. But it still involves feeling powerless. It just involves different *forms* of powerlessness.

EP: It does?

M: Sure! Look at the situations in which you smoke. In social situations, it's usually when you don't know what to say; at work, it's usually when you don't know what to do next; and at home, it's usually when you don't know how to occupy yourself. There are other situations, too, but if you examine them you'll find they all involve feeling powerless in some way or another.

EP: But there's *more* to my smoking than just feeling powerless! Sometimes I feel that I need to smoke just to relax—to relax physically, that is. I don't think all this is in my head. Some of it's physical!

M: As I mentioned earlier, what you feel *after* smoking is a separate issue from why you start to smoke.

EP: You don't think smoking relaxes me?

M: I didn't say that. Of course, smoking relaxes you. But so do lots of other things, like watching TV, for instance.

EP: No, I meant physically. Don't you think smoking relaxes me physically?

M: Yes. Smoking *does* relax you physically, but the tension you feel in your muscles just prior to smoking comes from feeling powerless, not from anything else.

EP: You mean to say that feeling powerless has a *physical* component?

M: Yes. Feeling powerless causes the muscles of your body to tighten. It makes your chest muscles contract. When you smoke, you inhale deeply and expand your lungs. That relaxes your chest muscles. You could get the same physical result by inhaling oxygen instead of cigarette smoke.

EP: That's really hard to believe. (Pause) Why does feeling powerless make my chest muscles contract?

M: It's a natural response. Just like a cat tensing its muscles when threatened by another animal.

EP: But I'm not threatened by another animal. What am I threatened by that would cause me to contract my chest muscles?

M: Loss of control.

EP: Loss of control?

M: Yes. Whenever you're afraid you won't be able to control some future event—something your Parent says you *should* control—you restrict your breathing.

EP: But why would I do a thing like that?

M: Because when you control your breathing, it *feels like* you're controlling events.

EP: That's really amazing! You're saying that when I'm afraid of losing control I always hold my breath, and tighten the muscles around my chest, all to make myself *feel* I'm gaining control?

M: Yes. Remember earlier when I said that fear wasn't a feeling, like you thought it was?

EP: Yes.

M: Do you remember what I said that fear was?

EP: You said that fear was a method of using energy.

M: Right. What happens is that when you feel powerless, you put tension into certain of your muscles. You do this by withdrawing energy from the part of your body that becomes tense—in this case, your lungs.

EP: I do?

M: Yes. Energy flows freely only when you're relaxed. The way you create tension is to restrict your energy flow.

EP: That's a little hard to understand.

M: Look at it this way. When a cat's threatened by something, he restricts his energy flow by tensing his muscles, preparing to release that energy in a big burst, so that he can spring to safety.

EP: Oh. Okay.

M: Well, the same thing happens to *you* when you're threatened—except that when you were threatened when you were young, and put in a powerless position, there was nowhere to spring to.

EP: So what did I do?

M: You kept the tension in your muscles. After a while your muscles became chronically tense and resisted your natural efforts to relax them. The result was that you stopped yourself, both mentally and physically, from doing what you wanted to do, from being yourself, and from becoming fully energized.

EP: But why would I *keep* my muscles tense?

M: Tension became locked into your muscles just as your Adapted Child feelings became locked on tape in your head. Constant exposure to the same powerless situations in growing up caused your mind, as well as your body, to lose its resilience. When you reached the point where you could no longer stop your Adapted Child tapes from playing automatically, you could no longer keep your muscles from tensing, either.

EP: So the body and the mind work hand in hand?

M: Yes. The body is really a reflection of the mind.

EP: Okay. So if I tie this all back to my smoking, the reason I smoke is that I start feeling powerless in some way and tighten my chest muscles. As I become aware of feeling slightly anxious, I start to smoke. Then, as I smoke, my chest muscles relax, and I feel more powerful again.

M: Very good.

EP: The problem in the past has been that I *thought* I smoked to relax. I connected the reason for my smoking with what happened afterward, not with what happened *before* I started to smoke.

M: Right again.

EP: Okay, now. I've got that straight. But there's still something bothering me. It seems I've got to work on two separate things. First, I've got this old pattern of wanting to feel victorious whenever I feel anxious; and it's tied in with smoking, and putting one over on my parents because they wouldn't give me permission to smoke. It's part of a repeating powerless cycle, where I trick myself into thinking that feeling victorious is feeling powerful.

M: So far so good.

EP: But I've also got this other problem of making myself feel anxious at various times because underneath it all I'm really feeling powerless.

M: You're *making* yourself feel powerless.

EP: (Pause) Okay. Yeah. That's right. I'm *making* myself feel powerless.

M: So what's the problem?

EP: Well, how do I deal with these two separate issues?

M: You deal with them separately. You decide to give up the need to feel victorious when you feel powerless, and you decide to examine each moment of powerlessness separately, to determine what you're saying to yourself, and what Parent tape is playing that needs to be turned off. Then you decide to turn it off.

EP: And when I do both those things, will the final decision be automatically reflected in my muscles, so that I'll also be physically relaxed?

M: Not always. Your muscles have had years to lock into position. But if you don't relax automatically, you can use physical means, like breathing deeply, to deal with your muscles.

EP: Whew! This has really been complicated, but I finally understand myself a lot better than I did before. Now I know why giving up smoking is so difficult for most people!

M: Are you going to stop smoking?

EP: I'm going to work on it, and watch for the different ways I make myself feel powerless. I think if I just work on them one by one, I'll reach the point where I won't *need* to smoke any more.

M: That's a good start. You may still need to make a separate decision about smoking somewhere on down the line, but it will be an easier decision to make once you've got the whole process under control.

EP: Okay. Are we finished for now?

M: I am, unless you've got something more to say.
EP: No, I don't. I'm exhausted!
M: Okay. See you later.

Comments

1. If you've already had some success in learning to see clearly, and if you've done some work on regaining your power, you've probably noticed that you no sooner shore up your power in one area than it begins slipping away in another. If you deal effectively with your eating habits, you may start smoking more. If you stop smoking, you may put on weight. If you stop spending money recklessly, you may start philandering. It's as if your body is a container, leaking energy, and once you plug up one hole, your power (or energy) starts leaking out another.

This situation is very common. It occurs, essentially, because your mind and body are not yet in equilibrium, and you still have many Adapted Child feelings left on tape. As you give up one type of adapted behavior (particularly if it was very important to you), you may begin feeling deprived and try to compensate by substituting another. You won't, unfortunately, start substituting *Natural Child* behavior and feelings until your Adapted Child tapes are almost all eliminated (or replaced). Natural Child feelings are usually too tentative to have the strength to compete with more familiar, and stronger, Adapted Child feelings. The existence of these Adapted Child tapes will continue to constitute "holes" in your internal power "container" until you've actually eliminated them.

2. This isn't a book on physical therapy, but certain aspects of the relationship between the mind and body are important for you to know. In the process of making early decisions about how to run their lives (and recording these decisions in their Parent and Adapted Child), people often record decisions *in their bodies,* by permanently tightening certain groups of muscles! (Tightening a muscle causes a

person to stop using it freely, and brings that muscle under the direct control of his Parent and Adapted Child.) Severe energy blocks caused by disagreements between the Parent and Natural Child, or between the Adapted Child and Natural Child, may be physically maintained throughout a person's lifetime by chronic muscular tension.

The decisions hardest to change are frequently those locked in the muscles of your body. You may redecide these decisions *mentally,* yet still be left with physical programming that causes them to linger well beyond the point when they might normally disappear. Some muscles may continue to send messages to your emotional system even though your brain no longer wants to receive them. They may continue to drain your energy, and sap your power, unless the stress patterns in your body are deliberately broken up and the tension released through direct physical manipulation.

Although information on exactly *where* decisions are recorded in the body is skimpy, it's been fairly well established that certain Parent messages and decisions are stored physically in and around the muscles of the shoulders. A person with tense shoulder muscles, a stiff neck, and a rigid back will usually have more difficulty dealing with his Parent (and ridding himself of his archaic Parent messages) than a person without such physical symptoms. Certain Adapted Child feelings—particularly fears, anxieties, and self-doubts—are stored in and around the muscles of the midsection (the "gut"). Chronically tense muscles in this area not only cause ulcers and other gastrointestinal difficulties, but also prevent a person from getting in touch with his Natural Child. (A "gutless" person has muscles so chronically distorted that he's constantly in the grip of some Adapted Child fear. A person who can't make good "gut" decisions has muscles so tense that he's cut off almost entirely from his Natural Child.) Other decisions we make are apparently stored in the muscles of our legs, our jaws, and as we saw in this chapter, our lungs.

If you reach the point in your personal growth where

your redecisions are simply not being reflected in your behavior, and in what you *feel* in your body, you might consider supplementing your growth program with some physical treatment plan to relax your muscles and open up your internal flow of energy. Treatment available in the United States includes:

(a) *Lomi Body Work*—A process that focuses specifically on releasing energy blockages in the body. Lomi practitioners physically manipulate muscles to *permanently* release chronic tension. The entire process requires a series of from ten to twenty sessions (of an hour each) over a period of six to twelve months. The sessions may occasionally be painful, because some very deep muscles in your body may be extremely tight, but they're *always* worth it. Practitioners of Lomi Body Work may currently be found in San Francisco and Houston. It's a new science (or art), and as new people are trained, they'll undoubtedly locate in other cities. My own experience has been with the Lomi School Southwest, which is run by Michael and Linda Smith. Their address is:

> Lomi School Southwest
> 1514 Missouri Street
> Houston, Texas 77006

(b) *Structural Integration* (sometimes called "Rolfing" in honor of its founder, Dr. Ida Rolf)—Though Rolfing goals are different from Lomi goals, some techniques are similar. The main goal of the treatment is to realign the human body in the gravitational field, so that people stand straighter, walk straighter, and get rid of certain physical ailments that have chronically afflicted them. Treatment is compatible with Lomi, though Rolfing will not completely untie your energy blocks. Consider it a second choice if Lomi isn't available in your part of the country, or if you're not able to travel to obtain it. (The sessions run for about the same length of time, and involve the same sorts of physical manipulations, as Lomi.) If you can't find a practitioner of Structural Integration in your local phone book, write:

> The Rolf Institute
> P.O. Box 1868
> Boulder, Colorado 80302

(c) *Yoga*—There are many goals in yoga. You can reduce muscular tension and make your body more supple through yoga exercises. You can also increase your energy flow through certain types of breathing exercises. The general physical and mental well-being yoga offers is compatible with both Lomi and Rolfing, although yoga requires more daily attention. To gain benefit you must usually plan on a daily commitment of at least thirty minutes. Many YMCA-YWCAs offer courses in yoga, and many yoga books are available to the interested reader.

CHAPTER EIGHTEEN

EP Stops
Resisting Himself

EP: Boy! Did I have trouble sleeping last night! I'll never get rich if I can't get a good night's rest when I need it!

M: What was the problem?

EP: Well, I had to be out of the house early this morning for an eight o'clock appointment. And whenever I have to get up early, I just don't sleep well the night before.

M: I heard your Parent say that you "had to" get up early.

EP: Hmmm. (Pause) I did say that, didn't I? Let's see if I can rephrase it.

M: No. Don't do that. Rephrasing your statement won't help.

EP: Oh? Why not?

M: You can't change the fact that your Parent's involved in your problem. Rephrasing your statement will only disguise your Parent's involvement.

EP: But I don't want my Parent to be involved. I want to explain this to you as clearly as I can!

M: If you explain it spontaneously, I'll be able to hear what the problem is. If you try to make it sound Adult, you'll disguise the problem.

EP: You mean you won't understand the problem if I use my Adult to describe it?

M: I won't *hear* the problem. Most of your problems stem from things your Parent and Adapted Child do that your Adult is not aware of. If you use your Adult to describe these problems, you'll keep your Parent and Adapted Child from surfacing, and I won't be able to hear them.

EP: But wouldn't it be *easier* for me to use my Adult to describe them?

M: Your Adult *can't* describe them! They occur outside its awareness.

EP: But it can describe them *partially*.

M: If your Adult understood your problems well enough to talk about them, they wouldn't be problems. Using your Adult to *try* to describe them only prevents your Parent and Adapted Child from speaking—which in turn prevents me from hearing how your Parent and Adapted Child might have caused the problems in the first place.

EP: But I thought I was supposed to use my Adult whenever I could. I thought I should *avoid* operating from my Parent.

M: You *are* operating from your Parent, whether you like it or not. If you want to get clear, your only choice is to hear what your Parent has to say, so you can decide whether or not you want to change it.

EP: You mean I *shouldn't* stop operating from my Parent and Adapted Child, even though they can be harmful?

M: No, I'm not saying that. I'm saying if you're in your Parent, you're in your Parent, and all the shoulds and shouldn'ts in the world won't change that fact. You don't have to *act* on the basis of what your Parent says, or on the basis of what your Adapted Child says. But you need to let their voices surface in order to learn what they're saying.

EP: Oh! (Excitedly) I think I see what you mean! You already heard my Parent say I "had to" get up early this morning, and you could tell that my Parent was involved in this problem in some way. And if I just keep on talking about the problem, using whatever part of me happens to speak, whatever's causing it will pop up spontaneously by the time I finish the explanation!

M: Right. And the solution will become apparent, also.

EP: Huh? (Pause) It *will?*

M: Yes. The solution to every problem is hidden in the description of the problem. You need only listen for it.

EP: Hmmm. (Thoughtfully) Yeah. I guess you're right. That's really the way we've been doing this all along, isn't it? As I've been describing each problem, you've been hearing the solution and pointing it out to me. Like, what tapes to turn off and such.

M: Yes.

EP: Funny. But I never quite thought of it that way. I never thought that the solution to a problem could be hidden in its description!

M: That's why *hearing* is so important. (Pause) But the burden for solving a problem falls equally upon both the speaker and the listener.

EP: What do you mean?

M: I mean that the person doing the describing has to allow his various parts to surface, and the person doing the listening has to hear them.

EP: Hmmm. (Pause) I think I see your point.

M: Okay, then. Do you want to stop having trouble sleeping?

EP: Yes, I do.

M: Then tell me what you *felt* last night when you were lying in bed and having trouble sleeping.

EP: Alert! I felt alert, and excited!

M: And how were you keeping yourself excited?

EP: Well, I just couldn't go to sleep, there were so many things running through my mind!

M: Like?

EP: Well, I was thinking I had to get up the next morning, and I didn't want to oversleep.

M: Were you *afraid* to oversleep?

EP: Yes.

M: After your *Parent* had told you that you had to get up early?

EP: Yes.

M: What part of you was afraid?

EP: Hmmm. (Pause) I guess it was my Adapted Child.

M: Were you responsible for getting yourself up in the morning, when you were young?

EP: Yes. (Pause) At least, I think I was. Let's see. I can remember my mother coming in and waking me, saying, "Aren't you up yet?" The implication was that I was supposed to be up—that I was supposed to get up by myself.

M: Did your mother ever say anything to you the night before about getting up the next day?

EP: I can't remember exactly. But it seems that on special occasions she might have said something like, "Remember, you have to get up early tomorrow."

M: Is that what you say to yourself now?

EP: Yes.

M: Did you have your own alarm clock when you were young, so you could wake yourself up?

EP: No. Not that I remember. (Pause) Well, when I was older, I did. But not until I was in high school. Before that, my mother always woke me up.

M: So when you were told to "remember" to get up early, you didn't have your own alarm clock?

EP: Yeah. That's right. It really doesn't make much sense. I wasn't actually responsible for getting myself up because my mother always woke me up; but I usually tried to do it by myself, anyway. And I worried about it.

M: Okay. What else were you thinking about last night when you couldn't get to sleep?

EP: I was thinking about the excitement of the next day—about getting up early and going on my appointment. (Pause) And I was thinking about the bad part, too; about having to get up and struggle around, half asleep, trying to make sure that I got out of the house on time.

M: Sounds like your Parent again—making "sure" you got out "on time."

EP: Yeah. I guess it was.

M: Anything else?

EP: Yes. I was also thinking about other things I just

wanted to think about. You know! *Fun* things! (Pause) Like, how I was really starting to take charge of my life, and how I was going to be rich and happy.

M: Were these thoughts exciting?

EP: Yes. Really exciting. It was almost as much fun as *being* rich and happy!

M: Do you normally do all this thinking before you go to sleep?

EP: No. Not if I don't have to get up early the next day. (Pause) That's the problem. If I don't *have* to get up early, I don't even think about it. I go right to sleep.

M: Why think about it just because you have to get up?

EP: (Thinking) Because I don't want to forget about getting up. I don't want to oversleep!

M: Your Adapted Child again?

EP: Yeah.

M: But that doesn't explain why you create the feeling of excitement. Let's see what *that's* about. (Pause) How did you feel this morning when you got up?

EP: Tense. I felt reasonably alert, but not really relaxed and sharp. I was tense. I needed more sleep, and my face felt like I hadn't awakened yet.

M: You didn't want to get up?

EP: Not at all. I felt miserable. I needed more sleep. It was too early to be up!

M: You were angry?

EP: Well, not that I . . . (Pause) Yes! I *was* angry! I was annoyed that my sleep pattern had been messed up. I've got an established sleep pattern, and I just can't wake up whenever someone says I should!

M: Who says you've got an established pattern?

EP: Me! It's *my* pattern! I ought to know whether or not I've got it!

M: How did you learn about your pattern?

EP: I've *never* liked to get up early!

M: You didn't answer my question.

EP: (Sounding annoyed) Well, I don't *know* how I learned about it! I do know I don't like people messing with it!

M: Even yourself?

EP: What do you mean?

M: If you *wanted* to get up early, would it be okay to mess with your pattern?

EP: I don't *like* getting up early!!

M: But if you *wanted* to?

EP: I wouldn't want to. I only get up early when I *have* to.

M: But *suppose* you wanted to. Just suppose. . . . Would you still continue to resist it?

EP: I can't picture the circumstances under which I'd want to.

M: You're resisting this very strongly. It sounds like the way you made this pattern your own was by resisting efforts to change it.

EP: (Thinking) That may be so, but the pattern *existed* before anyone tried to change it.

M: Has someone other than yourself tried to change it?

EP: Yeah. That's right! Certainly *I* didn't try to change it.

M: Is that when the resistance started?

EP: Yeah. I guess so. (Pause) But so what?

M: Suppose you'd decided to change it for yourself. Would there have been any need to resist the change?

EP: Well, I guess not.

M: But since it wasn't your decision—since it was someone else's—you *resisted*?

EP: Hmmm. (Pause) I'm beginning to see your point.

M: How did you learn about this pattern of yours in the first place?

EP: I've preferred sleeping late for as long as I can remember. I need lots of sleep.

M: You can get lots of sleep if you go to bed early.

EP: Yeah, but I've never liked going to bed early.

M: Oh? Did you have to go to bed early when you were young?

EP: (Spontaneously) Of course. All kids do. I had to go to bed even if I wasn't tired.

M: And what did you think about that?

EP: I didn't care for it!

M: (Pause) As a child, what did you do when you went to bed early?

EP: I don't know. I guess I'd just lie in bed and think about things.

M: And what did you *feel* when you were thinking about things?

EP: Alert. Alert and excited. (Pause) I thought about all the neat things I was going to do in the future. They never came true, but it was fun thinking about them.

M: Was the excitement you felt the same sort of excitement you felt last night when you were trying to go to sleep?

EP: (Pause) Hmmm. Yes. It was. I was thinking about the future.

M: And when you were young, what did you *feel* when you were made to go to bed against your will?

EP: Angry! I didn't want to go to sleep. I wanted to stay up with the grown-ups.

M: So. They made you go to bed, but they couldn't make you go to sleep, could they?

EP: Right!

M: Is going to sleep another power struggle for you?

EP: Power struggle? In what way?

M: Didn't you hear yourself speaking of your struggle with your parents?

EP: You mean about making me go to bed?

M: Yes. (Pause) Did you have any choice?

EP: No. I didn't.

M: And did you feel powerless?

EP: Oh! Wow! Yes! (Pause) And when I felt powerless, I immediately began to feel angry!

M: And how did you try to regain the feeling of power?

EP: (Eyes lighting up) Well, I just stayed awake!

M: And what did you *feel* while staying awake?

EP: Excited! Energized!

M: Powerful?

EP: In a sense. Really, I felt victorious! Like you said before, they could make me go to bed, but they couldn't make me go to sleep. In the long run, I won!

M: And now, when your Parent tells you to go to sleep, or to get enough rest, you re-create your early victories and keep yourself awake.

EP: God! That's it! You've hit it right on the head!

M: (Pause) Okay, now. Knowing all this, do you think you'll have any more trouble getting to sleep the next time around?

EP: No. I won't. I certainly won't keep myself up half the night resisting sleep in order to defeat my parents. I really feel confident about that.

M: Good. This might also help you with your energy problems. Sleeping well can provide you with greater energy during the day.

EP: This has sure been a big help! Thanks a lot!

Comments

1. As you become more skilled at spotting your ego states, you may find yourself trying to switch from your Parent to your Adult (or from your Adapted Child to your Natural Child) by sheer force of will. You may try to substitute Adult words for Parent words (or Natural Child feelings for Adapted Child feelings) without fully exploring how your Parent or Adapted Child surfaced in the first place. This approach never succeeds in eliminating your Parent or Adapted Child! It merely succeeds in thinly disguising them! You'll end up looking like someone who's in his Parent, but trying to act Adult; or someone who's depressed, yet pretending he's happy.

Whenever you find yourself in your Parent or Adapted Child and you want to move to a different ego state, you must first let your Parent or Adapted Child surface so they can be examined fully. Like it or not, they're a very real part of your personality. Denying they exist, by trying to gloss over them, will merely enable them to maintain their power over you and slow down your progress toward health and happiness.

2. The more you gain perspective about yourself, the more likely you are to discover personal habits that either drain, interfere with, or inhibit your internal energy flow. These may include your sleeping habits, your sexual habits, your eating and drinking habits, and any other things you do that use physical or emotional energy. Over a period of time you'll need to examine all of them. You can't afford to "leak" power at the same time you're trying to focus that power on becoming rich and happy.

As you learn to stay in touch with what you feel, you'll find your most productive moments occur when you're feeling several different "positive" Natural Child feelings simultaneously! Certain combinations of feelings will be more useful than others, and certain unproductive combinations will have to be examined and given up, just as if they were Adapted Child fears and depressions.

Feeling alert will not be useful to you if you're also feeling tense (as EP was when he woke up after not having slept well). Feeling relaxed will not be useful to you if you're also feeling lethargic. Feeling comfortable will not be useful if you're also feeling bored. The most productive combination is the simultaneous feeling of being relaxed, comfortable, alert, eager, energized, excited, and powerful. Any time you aren't feeling this way, preparing to feel this way, or examining how you stop yourself from feeling this way is time you're not using to reach the goals of wealth and happiness.

CHAPTER
NINETEEN

EP Finds
His Own
Answers

EP: You know, Martian, the more I think about what kind of job I'd like to have, the more confused I get.

M: Oh? How's that?

EP: Well, I've been used to working on a salary, and it occurred to me that not too many people get rich doing that.

M: Are you surprised?

EP: Actually, I never much thought about it.

M: Do you know how you've stopped yourself in the past from thinking about it?

EP: I never had any *reason* to think about it. I never thought I *could* get rich. Now that I'm starting to think about it, I've found that I really don't have much information.

M: So?

EP: So how *do* people get rich?

M: You tell me.

EP: Well, they certainly don't do it on salaries or hourly

222 Run Your Own Life

wages! Not very often, anyway. They'd have to save up a hell of a long time!

M: So how do they do it?

EP: (Looking blank) I just don't know.

M: Think of some examples. Think of some self-made men.

EP: Well, *I* couldn't be like those Greek shipping magnates!

M: Tell me what they did before you tell me why you couldn't be like them.

EP: Well, I don't know for sure, but I think they bought up surplus war ships and converted them to freighters or oil tankers. They had a brilliant idea, and borrowed money from some people to finance it. *I* couldn't think up an idea like that!

M: Like what?

EP: Like *that!* An idea of such value! One with such great potential!

M: What *part* of you couldn't think of it?

EP: I don't know. *No* part of me could think of it! I just couldn't do it! (Pause) (Thinking) Except . . . well . . . theoretically at least, maybe my Natural Child could do it, if it knew how. It's supposed to be the creative part of me. But *I* don't know how! I find it hard to imagine!

M: How did *they* do it?

EP: Who? The Greek magnates?

M: Yes.

EP: (Thinking deeply) They must have wanted to get rich *so bad* they could taste it. And they must have stuck with it and kept thinking about it until an idea came to them.

M: And what do you imagine that felt like?

EP: What? Dreaming up such an idea?

M: Yes.

EP: I don't know. Powerful, I guess. And creative. And fun!

M: Why would somebody want to be rich so bad he could taste it?

EP: I guess he just *knows* that he can do it and he has his mind set on reaching his goal.

M: You mean other things don't enter his mind?

EP: That's right. He doesn't let them interfere. He *knows* he can do it, so he just *does* it!

M: But he knows he can do other things, too. Why would he focus all his attention on getting rich?

EP: I don't know. It must have some strange attraction.

M: Does it have that attraction to you?

EP: Hmmm. (Pause) Well . . . no. At least, not yet, because I don't focus all my energy on it.

M: What do you think would be the attraction for a person who focused all his energy on it?

EP: It must produce some sort of fantastic feeling. Like being on marijuana, or something. Or maybe like sex.

M: Why do you say that?

EP: Because he devotes so much energy to it.

M: Do you think that this fantastic sensation is in *having* the money, or in arranging to get it?

EP: Maybe both, but probably more in arranging to get it.

M: What sort of thinking would produce such a spectacular feeling?

EP: I don't know. I've never experienced it.

M: What sorts of things do you think your Greek shipping magnates thought about, or focused on, to dream up their idea?

EP: They probably focused on what they *wanted,* which was to get rich. Then they saw these surplus ships, in the present, and they put this picture together in their mind with what they knew to be the future need for freighters.

M: What connection did they make between the present and the future?

EP: Value! They conceptualized the increase in value!

M: So. You're saying that when they saw those ships, in the present, and then visualized the future, they put it all together in their minds in terms of value?

EP: Yes. It was like the dawning of a brilliant awareness!

M: How were they able to focus so much energy on one idea?

EP: I'm not exactly sure, but probably it came from a combination of things.

M: Like?

EP: Like knowing that conceptualizing such things is one of the ultimate human powers—certainly one of the most valuable, and one of the most envied.

M: And?

EP: And knowing that once they could do that—once they could conceptualize value—they could have just about anything they wanted in the whole world!

M: And knowing *this* produced the exhilarated feeling?

EP: Well, I think it was probably everything put together. Knowing they *could* do it. Having an idea of *how* to do it. Finding a specific instance which might work out. Anticipating the results of its working out. And *feeling* that all rolled up into one big, powerful feeling.

M: So the thinking, and the feeling, were intertwined?

EP: Yes. And the real motivation was at the feeling level. (Pause) But one thing I don't understand is how they could focus all their attention on their goals, day after day, without their families and other responsibilities interfering.

M: What don't you understand about it?

EP: Well, I have so many distractions. I not only don't get support, I get *interference*.

M: In what way?

EP: When I talk to my family or friends about what I'm doing, they act as if they don't understand. It's like nothing registers. They act surprised, or confused, or bored; but never excited and supportive. And as a result, I have to use my energy to defend myself or to argue. I just can't concentrate on my plan to get rich.

M: So?

EP: So it strikes me that this doesn't happen to people who really *get* rich. It *couldn't* happen to them because it would be too big a drain on their energy.

M: So?

EP: So, I'm bothered by that!

M: Why?

EP: Because it means I've got a problem. Something isn't right about the way I'm going about things.

M: Okay. (Pause) What isn't right?

EP: I don't have any support!

M: What kind of support do you imagine your shipping magnates had?

EP: Well, they had people around them who would listen to their ideas, and maybe make constructive suggestions rather than downgrade their ideas or seem confused.

M: And how did the shipping magnates get that sort of support?

EP: Huh?

M: What did the magnates do, and how did they act, so that people would react to them that way?

EP: Hmmm. (Pause) Well, I guess they acted very forceful and self-confident. They probably ignored people who said foolish things! I'm sure they didn't *need* people around them who wouldn't contribute positively!

M: And what happened because of this?

EP: They got all the people around them to focus their energies on the same problems! And with everybody thinking in the same direction—instead of pulling against one another—they could come up with even better ideas. Ideas that were even more creative and more valuable.

M: Okay. And what kinds of conversations do *you* have with those around you?

EP: Arguments. (Pause) I'll say something about what I'm thinking, and people won't understand, or they'll just disagree. I'll try to get someone interested in an idea of mine, and the idea won't even register.

M: Why do you want to get people interested in your ideas?

EP: So we can discuss them!

M: What good is discussing them?

EP: Two minds are better than one!

M: Two minds are better than one *only* if both people are interested in the same subject. (Pause) I hear you trying to talk about things to people who weren't interested.

M: Hmmm. (Sadly) Yeah. I guess you're right. That's what I've been telling myself. (Pause) But is there anything wrong with that?

M: Do you want to do it?

EP: Well, I could *use* the stimulus of another mind!

M: And are these people providing this stimulus?

EP: No. (Looking resigned) (Pause) I guess I've been barking up the wrong tree, trying to discuss my ideas with my family and friends.

M: What have you been getting out of doing it?

EP: (Thinking) I've been trying not to lose them! I've been trying not to leave them behind, but it just doesn't seem to work.

M: What would happen if you stopped trying to make it work?

EP: Well, for one thing, they wouldn't have any hold over me. I wouldn't have any need to be with them.

M: And?

EP: It would be sad. (Pause) They'd probably be shocked! They're all in a little rut, and they think that I'm in the same rut with them, just *talking* about getting out without really doing anything about it. They don't realize that I *am* getting out of the rut, and offering them the chance to come with me!

M: Why not go ahead and move out of the rut for yourself, and let them make their own decision to come along if they want to?

EP: I will! I'm getting out!

M: But you're not out yet. What are you doing to keep yourself from getting out?

EP: (Pause) Oh! You mean I'm staying in the rut by trying to drag them out of it with me?

M: Yes.

EP: And I should just move out? By myself?

M: If you *want* to.

EP: Oh. Wow! (Pause) That would take a lot of courage!

M: Not if you want to get rich. It's *automatic* if you want to get rich. That's how you can find out who is planning to come along with you and who is planning to stay poor.

EP: (Looking surprised) You mean everybody separates themselves out by deciding whether to come along or not?

M: Yes. And when you let people take charge of themselves, you'll be able to focus your energy more fully on your own plan than on theirs.

EP: (Pause) You mean I've been focusing on *their* plans?!

M: That's what I heard you say.

EP: Wow! (Pause) I guess I have. (Speaking slowly) It's like I've been trying to drag them along, even if they don't want to come.

M: Do you want to stop doing that?

EP: That's really a hard one. I have so much invested in my family and friends.

M: That investment got you where you are. And now it *keeps* you where you are. You must be willing to give it up in order to move to a different place.

EP: I hear what you're saying, and I know it must be true, but I'm having trouble acting on it.

M: What troubles you is that you must give up something from your past in order to move into the future. This is another moment of clarity.

EP: Okay. I hear you. (Thoughtfully) I guess I'll need to think about it some more.

M: All right. (Pause) Do you remember how you stopped yourself from talking about your Greek shipping magnates?

EP: Huh?

M: You were talking about the Greek shipping magnates and you reached the point where you described how they must have experienced a sensational feeling. Then you stopped.

EP: I stopped myself?

M: Yes. *I* didn't stop you!

EP: Hmmm. (Pause) Well, I can't . . . oh! (Looking surprised) You mean when I started talking about how hard it is to get support from my family and friends?

M: Yes.

EP: I stopped myself from talking about the Greeks?

M: Yes.

EP: By changing the subject?

M: Yes.

EP: Hmmm. (Thoughtfully) I guess that *is* one way to do it . . .

M: (Pause) Would you like to talk some more about the Greeks and what they must have felt?

EP: Yes.

M: Okay. What aspect would you like to discuss?

EP: Well, I don't know. *You* brought the subject up!

M: No. I didn't. I asked you if you knew you had stopped yourself, and I asked you if you wanted to talk some more about the same subject. You said, "Yes," and I'm willing to talk about it.

EP: Well, I seem to have lost my train of thought. It *was* exciting at the time, but then I started thinking about how I didn't have any support system to help me focus my thinking, and I got lost.

M: Do you think the Greeks needed help in focusing their thinking?

EP: Well, yes. Didn't they?

M: If the feeling they felt was as sensational as you suggested, wouldn't they just turn it on by themselves?

EP: Hmmm. You've got a point there.

M: What's the most sensational feeling you've experienced?

EP: Well, *sex,* I guess. And sometimes listening to music. I like to listen to beautiful music and look at beautiful things.

M: And what do you *feel* when you listen to music or look at beautiful things?

EP: It's hard to describe. Relaxed, sort of. And being calm and peaceful. I really enjoy it.

M: Does it feel powerful?

EP: Not particularly.

M: So, the best feeling you have in your life is different from the best feeling the magnates had, when they were feeling powerful just *thinking* about getting rich.

EP: Yes, I guess it is.

M: Do you want to do anything about that?

EP: What could I do?

M: What do you *want* to do?

EP: (Pause) I want to feel that really powerful feeling of creating wealth, of creating something of *value!*

M: Good. *Will* you feel it?

EP: Yes!!

M: *When?*

EP: Well, I'm going to start right now, and I'm going to keep the feeling with me for as long as I can, and when I lose it, I'm going to be aware of how I prevent myself from keeping it, and then I'm going to get it back.

M: Very good. What do you feel right now?

EP: Energized!

M: And what are you thinking about?

EP: I'm thinking about all the ways people can conceptualize value! They can take something of little or no value, and visualize how it could be *made* valuable. They can construct a picture in their mind of what it would look like, altered so that people would want it. They can also take something that already has some value, but is *increasing* in value—or has some additional value that its previous owner didn't know about—and they can buy it and hold onto it until the increase has taken effect.

M: Very good.

EP: And all of this entails having information about what's available and what other people want, or could be persuaded to want!

M: And how can you *get* that information?

EP: By looking for it, and knowing it when I find it!

M: (Pause) Do you realize you worked this all out for yourself?

EP: Huh?

M: You didn't ask me any questions, and I didn't answer any. I asked *you* the questions, and you answered me from your fantasy trip about the Greek shipping magnates! Your road to riches is all in your mind. It's already *there,* waiting to come out.

EP: (Thinking) I guess I just have to learn to ask myself the right questions . . .

M: Right.

Comments

1. Fantasizing in detail about how successful people obtained their wealth—particularly about how they *conceptualized* what they later achieved—is one of the most important steps you can take in learning to conceptualize what you want to eventually achieve. Virtually everything anyone has ever accomplished in life was first *conceived in his or her mind,* by fantasizing about it. All your efforts at conceptualizing what you want will be accomplished by the sustained fantasy trips of your Natural Child, supported by unrestrained Natural Child energy. The more you fantasize about what successful people *feel* when they're working out their ideas, the closer you'll come to feeling it yourself!

2. It's important to associate with people who support your efforts to do what you want in life (so their Parent won't criticize, and their Adapted Child won't interfere with you), but it's particularly important to find people whose Natural Child will encourage and stimulate your own Natural Child in your quest for wealth and happiness. The more you surround yourself with people who can provide Natural Child energy to combine with your own, and the more you can fantasize with each other about the same subjects, the more efficient your own efforts to achieve success will be.

CHAPTER
TWENTY

The Martian
Leaves

EP: You know, Martian, I used to think of my Parent and Adapted Child as being the *bad* parts of me, but if I keep on reprogramming myself the way I've been doing, pretty soon they'll be *helping* me rather than hindering me!

M: How is that?

EP: They won't be pulling against me anymore! (Pause) I've always heard that once you had a goal in mind you should be persistent, and keep after it, until you achieved it. But I could never *do* that! Even if I knew what I wanted, my Adapted Child would soon get depressed and my Parent would start telling me to do *other* things.

M: So?

EP: So *now*, I'm beginning to program my Adapted Child with good feelings—feelings of energy and power. And I'm programming my Parent to keep reminding me to do what I *want* to do, and to keep telling me that I can get it if I stick with it!

M: And how does this help you?

EP: It keeps me focused on what I *want!* I used to be sort of . . . unsynchronized. Usually, I didn't know what I wanted, and if my Parent told me to be persistent, I'd just resist, because it didn't make any sense to me.

M: And now?

EP: Now, I start out by checking what I want *first!* Then, with all this reprogramming I've been doing, it makes more sense to me when my Parent tells me to be persistent. I don't need to resist anymore!

M: And do you feel more powerful?

EP: Yes! It's like I don't have as many drains on my energy. Although . . .

M: Yes?

EP: (Hesitating) I don't know quite how to say this, but every now and then I have a relapse.

M: Oh?

EP: Yeah. (Sounding disappointed) Like yesterday, I ate like a pig. And I hurried around and felt powerless and confused; and there just didn't seem to be anything I could do about it. I mean *really!* I tried examining how I was preventing myself from being clear and feeling powerful, and I just drew a blank.

M: Did it clear up?

EP: Yes. Today I woke up feeling a hundred percent better!

M: And what did you learn from this experience?

EP: Hmmm. (Momentarily stumped) I guess I learned that every time I take a few steps forward, I seem to *need* to take a step backward. I just can't seem to keep going steadily forward at the same pace.

M: And what would you like me to tell you at this point?

EP: Huh?

M: You had a reason for bringing this subject up. You wanted me to say something.

EP: (Thinking) Well, I guess I wanted you to tell me about these relapses. Like, are they normal?

M: (Pause) What would you ask yourself right now, if you were me?

EP: What?

M: I said, what would you ask yourself right now, if you were me?

EP: Hmmm. (Thinking) That's a hard one. (Pause) I

guess I'd ask myself what was so important about being normal.

M: And how would you answer?

EP: I'd say I don't know. I mean, that's what my Adapted Child would say. Then my Adult would say that being normal isn't necessarily very important, but having relapses certainly is.

M: And if you were me, how would you respond to that?

EP: I'd ask what was so important about having relapses?

M: And you'd answer . . . ?

EP: I'd answer that it was important because I shouldn't be doing it! (Pausing, and hearing what he just said) Hmmm. That sounds like my Parent.

M: Okay. Why not continue having a dialogue with yourself, just as you've been doing? Would you be willing to do that?

EP: (Intrigued by the idea) All right! I'll give it a try! (Gathering his thoughts) Since I just heard myself talking from my Parent, I think my Natural Child might speak up at this point and say I wasn't comfortable about having relapses. I didn't *enjoy* it! Instead of feeling energized, I felt hungry, and depressed, and powerless!

EP: (Speaking as M) Then I'd ask myself how I had arranged to feel this way.

EP: I'd answer, "I don't know. It just seemed to happen—as if it was part of my growth process."

EP: (Speaking as M) Then I'd ask myself what it was I wanted to know about my growth process that caused me to bring the subject up.

EP: And I'd answer, "Nothing." I'd reply that I really didn't want to *know* anything. I was just making a statement—an observation about my own growth process.

EP: (Speaking as M) Then I'd ask myself what prompted me to make the statement, if I wasn't interested in learning anything.

EP: And I'd answer that I was curious, because what was happening was different from what I'd expected. I thought that once I built up some momentum in getting myself clear, I'd be able to keep it going. I didn't think that my Adapted Child would surface all over again, almost worse than before! I just didn't *expect* it!

M: (Pause) And *now*, what would you ask yourself?

EP: (Speaking as M) I'd ask myself if I just heard my Parent speaking—talking about things it *expected* to happen, which is really crazy because I don't know anything about the growth process . . .

EP: And I'd answer, "Yes." My Parent was speaking because underneath it all I was really feeling scared—because this was different from anything I'd ever experienced. (Long silence) You know, Martian, all of a sudden I feel so clear, I don't have anything else to say . . .

M: You don't really need me anymore, do you?

EP: (Stunned) God! Oh yes! (Looking frightened) I can't do this all by myself, just because I did it once! That doesn't mean I can do it *all* the time! You'd better not *leave* me, because I've got a million and one things to learn yet! There are lots of things I still haven't worked out!

M: And if you were me, what would you ask yourself right now?

EP: (Pause) I'd ask myself what I was feeling . . .

M: And . . . ?

EP: I'd answer that I was feeling panicked!

M: Go on . . .

EP: (Speaking as M) Then I'd ask myself how it was serving me to feel panicked.

EP: And I'd answer that I was hoping you might *see* me panicking, and it might convince you not to leave.

EP: (Speaking as M) Then I'd ask myself if this sort of Adapted Child behavior was still useful to me.

EP: And I'd answer, "No!" And I'd realize that it probably wouldn't have much influence on you, anyway.

M: You're really clear, now.

EP: Yeah. I'd also realize that it was more useful to me to continue this sort of internal dialogue just like I'm doing. (Pause) You know, I just flashed on the thought that if you leave me all of a sudden, I'd really be a babe in the woods! I haven't finished working out my problems with money yet, and I'm certainly not happy a hundred percent of the time. But I keep saying to myself that whatever happens, I'd better learn this last skill about how to ask myself the kind of questions you ask me as quickly as I can, so I'll have something to hang onto if you leave.

M: And what's happened to your feeling of panic?

EP: (Pleased with himself) It's disappeared! I feel okay now, and I've done it all by myself. (Suddenly sober) But this thing about leaving me . . . you wouldn't do it, would you?

M: What would you ask yourself right now, if you were me?

EP: I'd ask myself if I was starting to scare myself again.

M: And . . . ?

EP: And I'd say, "Yes."

M: And then?

EP: Then I'd ask myself if I wanted to continue doing it. And I'd answer, "No." (Sounding concerned) But Martian, if you *do* leave, it would be so unexpected! I mean, in the beginning, you talked about this being a journey, and frankly, there are a million things I haven't worked out yet, and some really hard-core Adapted Child feelings—some really *scary* ones—I haven't worked through. I mean, God! What a place to leave someone! It's like throwing me overboard without a life raft!

M: Once you can ask yourself the same questions I might ask if I were here, you don't need me anymore. All I represent is clarity, and you *have* that clarity now.

EP: (Sounding worried) But how will I know I'm asking myself the *right* questions?

M: What would you ask yourself right now, if you were me?

EP: Huh? (Looking startled) God! You never give up, do you? I'd ask myself how I was scaring myself!

M: And your answer?

EP: I'd answer I was scaring myself by thinking that I don't really *know* what you'd ask! I can do it all pretty well, if

I just fantasize about what you *might* ask and focus on what I feel and what I want, but to know for sure . . . to actually know what you'd really ask . . . well, I could *never* know!

M: And what would you ask yourself, right *now*?

EP: (Speaking as M) I'd ask myself if my fantasies had worked well enough, so far.

EP: And I'd answer, "Yes."

EP: (Speaking as M) And then I'd ask how I was continuing to scare myself.

EP: And I'd answer that I'm thinking my fantasies won't ever be good enough—that I'll never know for sure if I'm asking the right question. (Looking surprised) I'm *doubting* myself!!

EP: (Speaking as M) Then I'd ask if I wanted to continue doubting myself.

EP: And the answer is "No," so I'll stop! (Pause) Wow! I'm beginning to feel like I'm climbing a ladder but I'm not bothered by the height! Going from one rung to the next simply isn't any problem—no matter how high I get!

M: Good. Now that you're feeling so confident, I'd like to hear what you plan to do to become rich and happy.

EP: Oh, yeah . . . (Pause) It seems so long aso when I first brought that up. (Looking reflective) Gee, I've really traveled a long way, haven't I?

M: Yes.

EP: Actually, I'm already a whole lot happier than I used to be. I have a sense of my own power, and I can really see what's going on around me. I've also eliminated a lot of old, useless, negative feelings. That's quite a bit, right there, when you think of it!

M: That's true.

EP: But I can become even happier by continuing to program myself to feel *good* feelings. I can hold onto them when I feel them, and they'll become even more familiar to me. And, of course, if I'm always doing what I *want,* and doing it the *way I want to,* I'll automatically be inducing good feelings!

M: Sounds okay to me. What about the riches part?

EP: Well, I *do* want to make lots of money, but at this stage I'm not too sure of the details. I know that sometime very soon I'm going to start fantasizing a great deal about what I might like to do that would also produce a good income for me. I'll also need to imagine how I'll *feel* when I succeed, so that I'll be focusing on success as an end product.

M: Excellent.

EP: You know, a person could get a super feeling like this almost any time, just by focusing on the fact that he has the power to do anything he wants! (Thinking) But I *still* have some questions for you, Martian, and I need you to answer them!

M: Ask the questions, and then answer them yourself, just as you've been doing.

EP: (Pause) Well, one thing I want to ask is how to tell the difference between a Natural Child "want" and an Adapted Child "want." I'm afraid that I'll stop myself from doing what my Natural Child wants by getting into my Adapted Child and wanting to rebel, or resist, or get revenge, or feel lethargic and just sit around and do nothing. And if I don't know it's my Adapted Child, I'll just *do* it!

EP: (Speaking as M) (Thoughtfully) I guess I'd answer by asking myself how I was continuing to scare myself.

EP: I'd reply that I'm scaring myself by concocting questions I don't know the answers to, and telling myself I have to know the answers, which, of course, I really don't. (Pause) At this point, *you'd* probably tell me I'll always be able to do whatever I want—and if some Adapted Child "want" is strongest, I'll just continue doing it until it doesn't serve me any longer. And you'd probably say it doesn't make any difference if I know whether it's adapted or not.

M: All right.

EP: (Frowning) Well, *would* you?

M: Would I what?

EP: *Say* that?

M: There you go again, doubting yourself. (Pause) But you know how to stop, if you want to. You really don't need any more help from me.

EP: I guess maybe you're right.

M: And since I'll be leaving soon anyway, I think I'll say good-by now. I won't actually leave until you're ready to say good-by to *me*, but from now on I'll only respond to you in one way: I'll ask you what you'd ask yourself if you were me. Good-by, Earth Person. I've enjoyed helping you get clear.

EP: (Looking stunned) No! Wait!! (Looking panic-stricken) Holy Christ!!

M: What would you ask yourself right now, if you were me?

EP: (Calming down) I'd ask myself how I was scaring myself, and the answer is that I'm starting to feel lonely, like I used to feel whenever someone left me alone when I was young. (Looking abandoned) But there are so many things I want to tell you, Martian. Like, how I've learned that the most important part of clarity is seeing inside myself. As I improve *that,* I automatically see better *outside* myself. (Voice drifting off) And there are so many things I still have to work out. So many things I have to learn. My Parent isn't going to be any help at all in figuring out how to get rich. I just don't have any useful information on it, really. Although now my Parent can see that I'm persistent. (Pause) Funny . . . just a while back I didn't *know* how much there was for me to learn.

M: And if you were me, what would you ask yourself?

EP: (Speaking as M) I'd ask myself what I was getting out of talking like this.

EP: And the answer is that if I didn't tell you all this before saying good-by, I'd feel unfinished. I've learned so much. And I appreciate it so much!

M: And if you were me, what would you ask yourself?

EP: (Speaking as M) I'd ask myself when I was going to stop saying how much I appreciated all this to someone who already *knew!*

EP: So I guess I'll stop doing it now. (Thinking) It's really amazing. I feel as if I've been sent out into the world again, just like when I first left home, but this time I've got the right information.

M: And if you were me, what would you ask yourself?

EP: (Speaking as M) I'd ask myself what I wanted to do.

EP: (Smiling) Ah! And now I've caught on to what you're doing! Your voice is already beginning to sound like a recording to me, repeating that same phrase over and over again—you've said it so frequently. (Nodding knowingly) "What would I ask myself if I were the Martian?" It's in my Parent now, and I guess I really don't need you anymore.

M: (Smiling but not saying anything)

EP: But I *did* need a voice from outside to keep reminding me to stay in touch with myself—one that I could put into my Parent so it would work hand in hand with my Adult and Natural Child. A voice I never heard when I was young . . . (Pondering a moment)

EP: (Looking around and seeing no Martian) Well, I guess he's gone. (Pensively) It seems strange, though. I don't feel at all abandoned. I feel he's a part of me. Hmmm . . . I wonder. . . . Could it be he always was?

Comments

1. The secret to becoming rich and happy is, of course, staying in touch with yourself. Once you've learned to do this—even though you may occasionally have relapses—you'll have a tremendous advantage over everyone else. Most people are so programmed to confuse themselves, to distract themselves, and to stay *out* of touch with themselves that they won't even know what you're doing.

If you find you need some more help in mastering this process, you might want to consider professional assistance. There are many specialists in the use of Transactional Analysis throughout the country. For the names of those nearest you, write to the:

International Transactional Analysis Association
1772 Vallejo Street
San Francisco, California 94123

But remember, just as in the world at large, there are members of the I.T.A.A. who are not very clear, who don't know what they feel, and who don't operate their lives on the basis of what they want (at least not very often). Others are very clear, and operate their lives much in accordance with the ideas presented in this book. They can help you immeasurably. You might want to talk to several members before drawing conclusions for yourself. If you've enhanced your perceptions from reading this book, you will easily distinguish the people who can help you from those who can't.